Ronald Fangen

Portrait of Ronald Fangen

Gyldendal Norsk Forlag, Oslo, 1946.

Ronald Fangen

✦

Church and Culture in Norway

Stewart D. Govig

Foreword
Bishop Per Lønning

iUniverse, Inc.
New York Lincoln Shanghai

Ronald Fangen
Church and Culture in Norway

Copyright © 2005 by Stewart Govig

iUniverse books may be ordered through booksellers or by contacting:

iUniverse
2021 Pine Lake Road, Suite 100
Lincoln, NE 68512
www.iuniverse.com
1-800-Authors (1-800-288-4677)

ISBN-13: 978-0-595-35441-2 (pbk)
ISBN-13: 978-0-595-79936-7 (ebk)
ISBN-10: 0-595-35441-6 (pbk)
ISBN-10: 0-595-79936-1 (ebk)

Printed in the United States of America

Christian humanism draws sustenance from a huge but often unknown company of people, past and present, who have talked, sung, written, and preached about human life imbued with divine reality.
—Joseph M. Shaw, et al, eds: <u>Readings in Christian Humanism</u>
(Augsburg, 1982).

Office of Church Relations
Pacific Lutheran University
Tacoma, Washington
2004

Contents

FOREWORD

It is not easy to sum up in a few sentences what Ronald Fangen (1895–1946) meant to cultural life in Norway and in Scandinavia as a whole. In many ways his influence can be compared to that of T. S. Eliot in England or Francois Mauriac in France. Because he belonged linguistically to a small minority on a world scale, however, he was excluded from the possibility of speaking from an international spectrum to his contemporaries as they did.

Ronald Fangen's decisive conversion to Christianity took place at a time when he had already gained a solid reputation as novelist. His was probably the most remarkable among the many conversions in Norway in the middle of the thirties as a result of the Oxford Group Movement's entry into the land. His Christian vision from then on, reflected in all his literary production, was no doubt determined by the world-conquering enthusiasm of "Buchmanism." But what he preaches is not a simple Oxford Group theology. It is a message strengthened and enriched by his strong feeling of Norwegian identity. His roots are in the Church of Norway and in the spiritual tradition indicated by Bishop Berggrav's famous periodical Church and Culture. A pietist in the sense that he insists upon the need for personal decision making and whole-hearted surrender, he opposes traditional pietism with its fear of the world and tendency towards isolationism.

From my early youth I remember one Sunday when our parish church in Bergen was so crowded that the doors had to be left open to permit those members of the congregation who were standing outside to hear the words from the pulpit. The man who preached the sermon that day was no ordained pastor. He was Ronald Fangen. His name meant more to Norwegian congregations than any hierarchical title or any theological degree. His voice was listened to as that of a prophet.

It is a pleasure for me to write this foreword to Dr. Stewart Govig's biography of Ronald Fangen. Through Dr. Govig's thorough and well-informed study, it is my hope that Ronald Fangen, the man as well as the message, will be really discovered by an American audience. Such a discovery will not only strengthen the ties between America and Scandinavia but also those which link Christians of various countries and traditions together. Rarely was a man with such strong national instincts less nationalistic than he. Rarely was a Lutheran Christian with such strong ties to his own Church less confessionalistic.

Fredrikstad, 6th December, 1971
Per Lønning, Bishop of Borg

ACKNOWLEDGMENTS (I)

Following the Second World War the 79th Congress passed the Fulbright Act which authorized an exchange of students, teachers, university lecturers, and research scholars with other countries. Grants provide roundtrip transportation and living expenses, payable in the currency of the host country, to support scholarly activities abroad for an academic year. Competition for Fulbright grants usually involves the applicant's selection of a topic of study, suited to his background and interest, and approved by the Selection Committee.

I was fortunate to receive a grant to Norway in 1957–58, having as my topic the religious views of the popular Norwegian author Ronald Fangen. During 1960–61 I returned to Norway with support from the National Lutheran Educational Conference and continued my research. Through its Board of College Education the American Lutheran Church granted me a "Faculty Growth" Award, and the Norwegian Research Council (Norges Almenvitenskapelige Forskningsråd) provided a grant for microfilming a number of Fangen's articles and papers.

During these years in Norway I met many persons who had known Fangen. Their insights, so freely shared, and the kindness they extended to me and my family are gratefully acknowledged. Their enthusiasm for my subject of study was a constant inspiration. At the close of a memorable afternoon spent with the late Bishop Berggrav I recall how he arose from his chair, walked over to a section of his library and returned with a small stack of books which I recognized to be Fangen's. Placing them on the coffee table in front of me, he exclaimed, "How I envy your task!"

My journey to Dusgård and the visit I had there with Solveig Fangen was one of the high points of my stay in Norway.

It is impossible here to name all the individuals who so willingly provided me with the resources necessary for my research, but I must certainly acknowledge a few without whom this brief biography could not have been written.

Einar Molland, Professor of Church History at the University of Oslo, took time out from the demands of teaching and writing to provide me with invaluable help in my research. The warm hospitality shown to our family by the Alex Johnson, Sigurd Lunde, and Peter Wilhelm Bøckman families made our stay in

Norway both productive and pleasant. Also particularly generous with their time and remembrances were Sten Bugge, A.H. Winsnes, and Carl Fredrik Engelstad. Here in this country Sverre Arestad, Professor of Scandinavian Languages and Comparative Literature at the University of Washington helped me enormously with his criticism and suggestions.

Kenneth O. Bjork, a former Professor of History at St. Olaf College, and Editor of the Norwegian-American Historical Association based in Northfield, Minnesota, also offered assurance. Although, he wrote, "this straightforward account of a remarkable person changed by the Oxford Group" was "outside the field plowed by the Association," it was surely "worthy of publication elsewhere" (Letter, September 8, 1972).

Without the encouragement of my wife who has so enthusiastically shared my admiration for Norway and its people this book would not have been written; to these—and others—credit is due for many corrections and improvements. The weaknesses and errors I accept as my own.

ACKNOWLEDGMENTS (II)

In 2002 Bishop Per Lønning visited the Pacific Lutheran University campus and lectured in the Scandinavian Cultural Center. It was a pleasure both to attend the event and visit with him afterwards. Since over thirty years had lapsed since we had discussed Fangen's authorship, I asked if people in Norway were still reading Fangen's books. "Not enough of them are," he replied. Hopefully this text will establish numbers on this side of the Atlantic to bolster the total.

During a recent meeting with Knut Vollebaek, Norway's Ambassador to the United States, the writer inquired about the subject of his study. "Fangen was a hero of mine in my youth," he replied.[1] Later he commented that Fangen's role in Norwegian cultural life was very important and made an impact long after his untimely death in 1946.[2]

Here on campus generous support and assistance were offered by Richard Rouse, Executive Director of the Office of Church Relations, and by Solveig Robinson of the English Department. Likewise, kudos to Carol Bucholz for typing and computer skills.

The cover photo reveals the Gokstad Viking ship bow replica located at the entrance to the University Scandinavian Cultural Center. The landscape beyond displays the campus Eastvold Hall Chapel steeple[3]. My thanks also to Evelyn Reynolds and SCC Director Susan Young for permission to employ a sketch of the photo scene.

Readers will note that upon engagement with this subject during the early 1970s, inclusive language was not in vogue. Please judge accordingly.

Stewart D. Govig
Professor of Religion Emeritus
Pacific Lutheran University

---

1. PLU Conference, "Pathways to Peace: Norway's Approach to Democracy and Development," Wang Center for International Programs, January 12–14, 2005.
2. Letter, February 1, 2005.
3. Jordan Hartman, University Photographer, 2004.

PREFACE

In the early afternoon of May 22, 1946, a war-weary German transport plane arose from Oslo's Fornebu Airport with eleven passengers and three crewmen aboard. Seconds after take off an engine faltered and the pilot desperately attempted a return to the runway. He failed, however, and in the resulting crash thirteen of the fourteen occupants were killed. Included among them was Ronald Fangen, at fifty-one a leading figure in Norway's cultural life, and one of the resistance heroes in the recently terminated Second World War's German occupation of Norway.

This book sets out to provide an account of his life, particularly for American readers who wish to learn more about the Christian backgrounds of their Scandinavian heritage. In recent years other biographies, such as Joseph M. Shaw's <u>Pulpit Under the Sky: A Life of Hans Nielsen Hauge</u> (1955), Alex Johnson's <u>Eivind Berggrav</u> (1959), and Charles J. Curtis' <u>Söderblom: Ecumenical Pioneer</u> (1967) have admirably served the same purpose. The following biography of a cultured twentieth century layman of the Church of Norway describes another dimension of this heritage.

Ronald Fangen (1895–1946) was an author who wrote as a novelist, dramatist, essayist, and literary critic. The scope of his writings is therefore wide and varied. The following work attempts to treat these writings within the context of Biblical and theological commentary. It is the first comprehensive and popular presentation of the basic facts of Fangen's life and the major themes of his religious views in the English language.

Chapter One, "Sun and Shadow," describes the turbulent early years of his life, and his first faltering attempts to write novels. Grounded in the tradition of his Church, he sought to enrich his faith by much reading and study on his own. Success came with the publication of the novels <u>Some Young People</u>, <u>Erik</u>, and <u>Duel</u> which reflected youthful search for truth following the devastating first World War.

Chapter Two, "Høsbjør," interprets the author's involvement with the Oxford Group Movement in Norway during the nineteen thirties. The Oxford Group, or Moral Re-Armament, is a skillfully directed religious movement which originated under the leadership of the American Lutheran clergyman Frank N.D.

Buchman. Its evangelism employed the "houseparty," a method of group persuasion quite similar to today's human potential movement activities. Buchman's followers have not only attempted to sway individuals but also legislative bodies; statesmen in the United States and in other parts of the world have been targets for Group propaganda. Among other countries in Europe, it entered Norway, where, in 1934 and 1935, it was remarkably successful. One Norwegian convert was Ronald Fangen. In his early writings, Fangen's religious views were intellectually oriented to the Christian religion. But as he matured, his relationship to Christianity developed into both an intellectual and an emotional commitment which resulted in the concerted effort he made to declare his Christian convictions in public during the closing decade of his life. An important reason for this change in attitude and conduct was his involvement with the Group. The impact of the Group crystallized Fangen's belief, which in turn led to his posture, in preaching and writing, as a "high class evangelical Christian."

The effect of the Group Movement upon the style and content of the author's writings is analyzed in Chapter Three, "Ferment in the Church." By this time active in the public life of the Church of Norway, Fangen became a popular speaker and effective apologist for Christian faith. He was often invited to speak before youth groups and came to be noted for inspiring insights regarding the manner in which the faith of a Christian might be applied in life. A Christian's life, he maintained, involved new opportunities for changed attitudes and activities; for him the new life of faith was a "day full of grace," and his search for new expressions of discipleship exemplified this attitude. Later on, his involvement in Church activities in Norway earned the respect of liberal and conservative alike.

Chapter Four, "Lengthening Shadows," describes the crises of imprisonment and illness which resulted from Fangen's participation in the resistance movement in Norway during the Nazi occupation of the land.

Americans who have a Scandinavian Lutheran background in their Christian heritage may agree that issues in the relationship between Christianity and culture today are perhaps more acute than during the times of our ancestors. Disputes within the life of the Church during seasons of culture wars, monetary crises, AIDS and terrorism reveal Fangen as prophetic in his intense concern for a better understanding of such tensions on the part of Christians. In his effort to relate the Lutheran heritage more positively to its community identity, Fangen described himself as a "Christian humanist." The style of this humanism and its implication to the Church are explored in Chapter Five, "Children of Light."

In a broad sense, as Jacques Maritain represents Christian humanism in France in a Roman Catholic society, and T. S. Eliot in Great Britain in the Anglican community, so also Ronald Fangen represents Christian humanism manifesting itself within a Lutheran Church tradition. From the Christian vantage today when, in proportion to the world's population gains, ours is a relatively shrinking faith, the challenge of secularism increases. The Christian humanism of Ronald Fangen may provide readers with another stimulus for reflective concern and response.

1

SUN AND SHADOW
1895–1934

o o o o o o o o o o o o o o o o o o o o o o o o o o o o o o o

"For we are but of yesterday...and our days on earth are a shadow."

—Job 8:9

1
SHADOWS OF THE FJORD

Probably no region in the world is more beautiful than the western coast of Norway. A maze of islands and mountains, the coastline features many arms of the sea called fjords which enable the Atlantic to reach deep into mountain valleys where they are frequently met by waterfalls cascading over the precipitous slopes. Some of these falls may be great and boisterous, while others, delicate and fragile, are shrouded in mist. Overhead the sun etches its mark along the wayside: dark shadows appear in mysterious mountain clefts, soft shades climb inland valleys, and, upon the water, pools of dazzling light come into view.

The play of shadows in a fjord suggests a perspective from which to view the major events of Ronald Fangen's life. He grew to manhood in the land of fjords, and by the close of his life was remembered by his countrymen for literary accomplishment and for his patriotism during the Second World War. But during this lifetime he also experienced events which traced patterns of sudden crisis and misfortune. In viewing these "shadows" the reader may discern various hues; upon reflection he may recognize similar shadows in his own experience and yet perceive, as Fangen did, the underlying truth that life is good.

The town of Kragerø is situated on Norway's picturesque south coast. Two of its citizens, Stener Fangen and his wife, Alice, had established a comfortable home there and were the parents of three sons. The father was a respected mining engineer. His wife, the former Alice Maud Lister, came from the distinguished English family which included Lord Joseph Lister. On April 15, 1895, a fourth son, Ronald, was born to them. Several years later, however, their marriage ended in a divorce. Alice Fangen, who remarried later on, became the manager of a hotel at Finse, while Stener Fangen moved to Vesteråle.

Five-year old Ronald was sent to live with two aunts in Bergen where he spent the remainder of his childhood years. He attended Hambro's School there, but because of poor health was unable to complete a formal education. This handicap, however, did not prevent him from learning on his own; he spent many hours reading literature, history, and philosophy at the Bergen Public Library. The novels of the Russian writer Dostoevsky had a special appeal to the intelligent adolescent. Remarkably mature for one his age, Ronald had delivered a public address, "Our Language" (in nearby Voss) at the age of fourteen. Attending Church services regularly, he grew to love the Lutheran liturgy and hymnody.

The sermon summations he gave to his aunts led them to comment that it was now hardly necessary for them to attend Church themselves!

Sudden tragedy marred these childhood years when a favored elder brother, Stener, after having been accused of cheating in a school exam, committed suicide in the very room he shared with Ronald. The accusation proved groundless, yet to one of Stener's sensitive nature, it became too much to bear. His younger brother was deeply disturbed that his own precocious performance at school had made him a cheating suspect as well; he also had considered ending his life. The shock of Stener's death may account for the repeated discussions of suicide which appear in Fangen's novels; such discussions became a feature he ponders in his works perhaps more than any other Norwegian writer.

The separation of his parents, a fragile condition of health, and Stener's tragic death brought early maturity. A literary critic, Paul Gjesdal, writes of Fangen's having grown up "without a childhood" when he commented:

> Not only musical prodigies are to be found. They are the most common, but science and literature also have theirs. There are some young persons who have hardly had a time of youth and hardly any childhood, plants that shoot up rapidly. There are children with tired eyes, who by the age of twelve have their religious experience behind them and by the age of sixteen have read and partially understood Kant's critique of reason....[1]

In a letter to the editor of a Bergen newspaper the youthful Fangen's interest in Christian faith and its relationship to the secular is apparent:

> A great mistake of Christians has always been that they have withdrawn from life and become indifferent to culture. We Christians should understand the times and not flee to the mountains and hills. Life gives us opportunities, goals, and God gives us means. Therefore, we should deepen our interest for all men, attempt to understand our times and mould them—as Christians.[2]

He did not appreciate a self-satisfied type of Christian which was antagonistic to human cultural life. "How unchristian it is," he wrote, "to judge so many outside the faith."[3] The Christian humanism of the youth is implied in his earliest writings; he insisted that despite all the "guilt for sin" we know so well, our humanity can become something not to lament but rather to acclaim.

In the spring of 1913, Fangen sailed for Argentina. The reflective nature of the eighteen year old is shown in a poem he wrote about the long voyage at sea: "We were gripped by a feeling of eternity."[4] Arriving in Argentina, he lived with a brother and visited the vast plains country; while there he "sat on horseback trying to write poetry," he related to a friend.[5] He also occupied this time by writing a series of travel articles for an Oslo (then called Kristiania) newspaper before returning to his homeland several months later.

Traces of these "shadows"-the broken home, a brother's suicide, and poor health-would follow in the years to come. But the sensitive youth would never lose sight of the view of human existence as a gracious gift, and free obedience to Jesus Christ as a path for discovering his own humanity.

2
STARTING A CAREER

Having moved from Bergen to Oslo, Fangen became a reporter for the paper The World Today (Verdens gang) and (at the age of nineteen) was appointed editorial assistant of the periodical The Week's Review (Ukens revy) in 1914. His political commentaries and literary reviews established his reputation and opened the door to a new circle of intellectual friends such as Nils Kjaer, Carl Naerup, Sigurd Bødtker, and Olaf Bull. From the many hours of conversations with them he developed his broad humanism and thirst for a literary career. These representatives of the Oslo literary milieu became his teachers and introduced him to the Christian humanist tradition of European culture. Fangen's essay collection Reconnoitering in Literature and Philosophy (Streiftog i digtning og tænkning, 1919) which includes studies of Dostoevsky, Carlyle, Weininger, and Wells is a measure of his indebtedness to them.

The teenage journalist was not content with the work of literary criticism; he wished to become a writer himself. In fact, by 1911 he had completed his first novel which was published in 1915. On July 17 of that year he was married to Solveig Brandt-Nielsen.

The Weak (De svake), was published when the precocious writer was only twenty. In this novel he evaluates the world's crisis of war in a surprisingly mature manner for one of his age. Terje Gude, the leading character, sees his ideals shattered to pieces in the crisis of the times but this experience enables him to get "behind" the materialistic and secondary factors of life to view its real conflicts. These conflicts are overpowering and make the person who experiences them "weak". Yet such a person has a deeper and more intensive experience of life. At the beginning of his career Fangen was influenced by Nietzsche and reveals a deeply serious and somewhat pessimistic outlook on life. This outlook is also seen in the novels which followed in rapid succession, One Generation Gives Birth to Another (Slægt føder slægt, 1916), A Novel (En roman, 1918), and Crisis (Krise, 1919).

None of the novels won critical acclaim or a popular following. When compared to the more mature and successful novels Fangen wrote later in his career, they appear to be tentative and experimental in nature. Perhaps for this reason there are aspects of them which offend the reader: the unlikely, lengthy conversations and diary excerpts, the unreal development of characters and their connections with one another, and the sometimes abrupt, artificial scene changes. The background of violence and the intense seriousness of the narratives become tiresome. Deaths occur in an atmosphere pervaded with doom, and the suicides of Gottfred Harm in The Weak, George Storypta in A Novel and Major Alm in One Generation Gives Birth to Another foreshadow the grim theme which would be repeated in later novels. In these early novels, descriptions of tragic home backgrounds are the rule rather than the exception, a feature which in all likelihood reflects the author's own unhappy childhood. The four early novels are not included in the author's collected works. In retrospect it is easy to understand why they were excluded.

Toward the close of the War, the young journalist accepted an invitation to become a co-editor of the new Scandinavian literary journal Literature (Litteraturen). As a consequence, he moved to Denmark for several years. Two daughters were born to Solveig and Ronald Fangen during these years and it was at this time that the aspiring author made his first literary breakthrough. At the urging of his wife, Fangen attempted to write in a different form—drama—and the play Fall into Sin (Syndefald, 1920) premiered at Oslo's National Theatre in the fall of 1920. When the critic Nils Kjaer had finished reading the second act, Mrs. Fangen recalled, he turned to her and remarked, "Do you realize you have married a dramatist?" Other critics were generous in their praise.[6]

The principle characters of Fall into Sin are the Lutheran pastors, Nils Gade and Olaf Årvik. As schoolmates, Årvik's Christian convictions had been an inspiration to Gade. Years later, Gade served as Årvik's parish assistant. In contrast to his friend, who accepted Church doctrines quite literally, Gade struggled with theological doubts (pp. 10–11).[7]

The second act of the play discloses Gade's relationship to Nini, Årvik's wife. Gade had loved Nini during student days and he now suspects she does not love her husband; therefore, he decides to renounce his profession and "accept the world" by asking her to go off with him. In his plea to Nini that she leave her husband, he maintains that both of them have been dominated by Årvik's rigid morality and have denied their emotions for too long a time. She agrees with Gade (pp. 27–45).

Act three occurs on the following day. Nini and Gade stand in the churchyard adjoining the building where Årvik is delivering his first sermon to the new congregation in his charge. Nini has become conscience stricken and afraid at the turn of events. Just then a man hurriedly leaves the church building, greatly distressed about the sermon. When Nini and Gade demand to know the reason, he explains that the pastor has confessed to his congregation that, as a youth, he had raped a girl. Årvik makes the shocking disclosure because he wishes to testify how, as a result of this experience, God's promise of the forgiveness of sins had become meaningful to him. Confessing this to his bishop before preaching the sermon, he cries out:

> To the depths of my terror and despair
>> God sent me his son to give His peace…
> I am the greatest among sinners and He has raised me up. He is the
>> sinner's God (p. 57).

Suddenly Gade and Nini realize Årvik is not perfect; he also has struggles with a "fall into sin." The play closes as Årvik forgives them.

The religious view of the play is suggested by the narrative of the "fall" in the third chapter of Genesis. In this well-known account, Eve, tempted by the serpent, eats of the fruit of the tree from which God has forbidden her to eat upon penalty of death. Pleased with the fruit, she shared it with Adam. Thereupon they became aware of their nakedness and attempt to hide from God. These reactions to their disobedience suggest their sense of guilt. Then God summons them and pronounces his punishments upon the serpent and upon Adam and Eve.

In terms of myth, Adam's "fall" may be viewed as the description of every man as a sinner before God the Creator. Although created good and free, man abuses his freedom and falls to the temptation of pride and selfishness: this in turn leads to his estrangement from God. Yet, according to the Biblical narration, God did not abandon Adam and Eve. His judgment upon them was a means of awakening them to the realization of their separation from the source of true life, namely, fellowship with God. According to the New Testament, God's reconciling activity has culminated in the life of Jesus and the establishment of the Church.

The portrayals of Nils Gade and Olaf Årvik reveal the tension in the author's viewpoint concerning the Christian theology of sin. On the one hand, he pictures Gade as a humanist, who, in a self-reliant attitude, searches for new and meaningful values, while at the same time identifying himself as a Christian. On the other hand, Årvik relied upon God to provide such values; faith in God is his supreme value. Gade had discovered that his actions belied his motives, that the appearance of his outward self and the reality of his inner self bore no resemblance. So he decides to defy a moral standard of his Church because he wishes to be free from pretension. Before his decision to ask Nini to leave her husband, his outward relationship to the Church had prevented the expression of his desire to indulge in what excited him. His action is an assertion of a pride which he believed to be his right as a human being. But his new freedom, once experienced, does not bring him happiness. At the climax of the play he becomes aware of his self-centeredness and senses an inner weakness, a "fall into sin."

Årvik suppresses his own "fall into sin." Having never been assured of God's forgiveness of his sin as a youth, he attempts to atone for his guilt by becoming a pastor. Although he claims to trust in God's forgiveness, his real release comes only when he publicly declares his guilt before those who looked to him as a model for Christian faith and life. He learns that sin affects all men, including the moral and the faithful. Release from the guilt caused by his terrible deed did not come from the performance of good works and the profession of religiosity; rather, it comes when Årvik makes a total acceptance of God's forgiveness.

In Fall into Sin Fangen upholds the dignity of human life, even in its struggle with sin. Årvik represents an irrational guilt feeling in man which distorts this dignity. Thus the Christian view of God's reconciling activity in dealing with man's sin appealed to the author; because God accepts man in spite of the distortion created by his sin, he can acknowledge life as a precious gift from God and set himself to the task of living a worthwhile life.

By 1921, Fangen had come to live at Hvalstad in Asker, a suburb of Oslo. While living there he took an active part in the cultural life of the capital city. As a literary critic and now as a writer himself, his chosen career challenged new efforts to write. Three daughters were born to Solveig and Ronald Fangen, and the family continued to live at Hvalstad until, in the spring of 1938, they moved north to Dusgård, near the resort town of Lillehammer.

3
OUR WORLD

In 1923 Fangen was appointed editor of the periodical <u>Our</u> <u>World</u> (<u>Vor ver-</u> <u>den</u>). Through this journal he entered upon a vigorous discussion of social and political issues in Norway and the rest of Europe during the decade following the First World War. To understand his attempt to analyze these issues, reference to some of the important trends in the history of Norway during this century is necessary.

When Norway gained full independence from Sweden in 1905, her government continued to develop and to extend the democratic practices for which a foundation had been laid in the nineteenth century. King Haakon VII proved to be a faithful guardian of democracy and he became the living embodiment of the free nation. Parliamentarianism enabled the people to enjoy a close contact with their government: "Democracy in Norway was not a mere form but an active reality."[8]

In the time from 1905 until 1940 Norway also enjoyed a long period of peace which contributed to the progress of the country. The population rose to nearly three million, and the economic life was marked by an increased industrialization as the nation's great resource of water power was developed for the needs of a growing industry. This meant that Norway would cease to be an essentially farming country. Industry drained labor away from the farms which resulted in the almost complete disappearance of the tenant farmer. As with industry, agriculture also initiated a program of modernization.

In cities the working people often lived in crowded tenement houses and nearly everywhere faced the possibility of exploitation by long hours and low wages. Aspirations for higher living standards gradually united the farmer in the country and the working man in the city, for wage and price competition had often been ruinous to farmers. Their common needs resulted in a social progressiveness which had a decisive influence upon Norwegian politics. The decade following 1905, therefore, was marked by increased social legislation.[9]

Whereas before 1905 the cause of independence from Sweden had been uppermost in the Norwegian consciousness, after 1905 economic and social questions became dominant. Compulsory health insurance became law in 1909, and accident insurance for seamen followed in 1911.[10] Such social legislation was based, to a large extent, upon the idea of the solidarity of the citizens of the nation. This movement had received inspiration from French social radicalism and from English liberalism. Because of the burden social legislation placed upon business and industry, it was opposed in conservative circles. In the nineteen thirties, however, social legislation was substantially increased and came to be generally accepted. This accounts for much of the national solidarity with which the Norwegians faced the German invaders at the time of the Second World War.

After 1905 the Labor Party began its rise to power. As the wave of revolution began to break over Europe in the closing months of the First World War, its effect was felt in Norway where the more radical elements took control of the Labor Party. These radicals desired the nationalization of industry, banks, transportation, and trade. But the Party split on the issue, and the radical half joined the Soviet Comintern in 1919. This group broke its tie with Moscow in 1923; a new split in the radical wing of the Labor Party formed the Norwegian Communist Party.

By 1935, however, the Labor Party had gained almost half the seats in Parliament. The following year, old age pensions were established. Efforts were made to permit farmers to control production by the formation of a national board to adjust prices and profits. The Labor Party continued to introduce more social legislation to improve the material conditions of the people and it was still in power when Norway was invaded in 1940.[12]

Fangen's commentaries during these years are recorded in the periodical Our World. This periodical was begun in 1923, with Fangen as its first editor. Norway's social structure was "...worth defending," he wrote, "and the periodical's so-called conservative point of view cannot be denied."[13] Human beings, he maintained, were not merely social creatures, and he argued against the claim of collective responsibility, for each person was to assume his unique place in society. Both Communism in Russia and Fascism in Italy, he insisted, had subjugated the individual's integrity in favor of the collective.[14] In addition, he informed his readers that because Communism was a religion it stood opposed to Christianity and maintained that this aspect of Communism should be exposed more in Norway:

> Communism is a born enemy of our culture, morals and religion, just as much as it is a born enemy of our social structure.[15]

In the face of Communism's threat to Christianity, Fangen criticized the lack of unity among the Christian people of Norway as exemplified in the disagreements between the policies of the State Church and the Inner Mission organizations.[16] His opposition to developments in Russia during the nineteen twenties lends weight to Kristian Elster's assertion that, following the First World War Fangen was a "Christian conservative humanist."[17]

Norway emerged from the War as a creditor nation, rich in money, but lacking in raw materials. This situation led to a harmful inflation. The value of the crown fluctuated and, by 1927, unemployment had reached alarming proportions. The luxury of the wealthy became more and more evident; while their living standards rose, those of the workers fell. On the international scene it appeared that the Allies had failed to bring social and economic stability.[18]

Begun in 1921, the periodical Toward Day (Mot dag) was the leftist counterpart to Our World. Under the leadership of Erling Falk, it became the organ of expression for radical intellectuals such as Nils Collett Vogt, Cora Sandel and Olaf Bull.[19]

> Christianity preaches compassion for the small and mistreated in society. Not compassion, we answer, but justice is their right…We unite with the workers to build up a new and better society.[20]

These words of the periodical's first issue set the tone of the Toward Day group of youthful intellectuals who worked for the periodical, including the authors Sigurd Hoel, Helge Krog, and Arnulf Øverland. Until the group disbanded in 1936, it exerted a powerful influence among students as it proclaimed a leftist view in the debate over Norway's social and political needs.[21] In Our World Fangen opposed the viewpoint of these literary colleagues until his periodical folded in 1931.

In 1930 Fangen wrote that his work as editor had involved considerable effort and that he wished to concentrate more in a literary direction. Victor Mogens succeeded him.[22] Fangen's contributions to the periodical had established his reputation as an intelligent interpreter of the spirit of the times in post-War Norway and in the rest of Europe. His critical appraisals had been incisive and his concentrated emphasis was upon what he maintained was the Communist movement's effort to impose an outside stimulus to Norway's development into a modern nation. In contrast, he believed this development should be an orderly and organic process.

Fangen had followed the Christian orientated humanism of Nils Kjaer and Helge Rode. He was perhaps the most outspoken among a group of other writers in close agreement with his individualism and his insistence upon a harmonious development of society, namely, Charles Kent, A.H. Winsnes, Sigurd Christiansen, and Sigrid Undset. Their point of view was given in the essay collection selected from <u>Our World</u> entitled, <u>The Dividing Line</u> (<u>Skillelinjen</u>).[23] When <u>Our World</u> ceased publication, this group of conservative humanists lost a rallying point.

4
A GROWING STATURE

In addition to the impact of the Communist movement in Norway following the First World War, the new concepts of Freudian psychology, biological evolution, and Biblical criticism began to rock the Church in Norway. The periodical Church and Culture (Kirke og kultur) provides a lively commentary to the Church's response to these new ideas during the post-war years. It was edited during these years by a young churchman, Eivind Berggrav, who was destined to become primate of the Church of Norway during the Second World War and a leading figure in its life during the first half of the twentieth century.[24]

Church and Culture sought to help Christians relate themselves in a positive way to these new intellectual views, and to establish points of contact with them. Thus Fangen praised Berggrav for his "open" attitude which was not bound by traditional "theological cliches." Berggrav's warmth and spiritual concern, he felt, could help believers find a deeper faith.[25] Later on, especially during the Nazi occupation of Norway, Fangen and Berggrav became close friends. Fangen also admired another youthful churchman, Kristian Schjelderup (who later became bishop of the Hamar diocese) and praised him as a "liberal theologian...who could be a blessing for the Church of Norway."[26]

Carl Fredrik Engelstad summarizes Fangen's intellectual posture at this time as a "liberal humanist with a Christian orientation."[27] The Christian orientation to which he refers was focused strongly upon the Church of Norway's liturgy and hymnody, a tradition the author deeply admired. In a Christmas meditation he even speculated that such a Church festival might help Christian faith to prevail eventually during the time of doubt and turmoil which had resulted from Communism's attack upon the Church.[28] Fangen's Christian orientation is also evident in his work as a writer, with the publication of Some Young People (Nogen unge mennesker) in 1929 and its sequel, Erik, in 1931. With these works he achieved his first success as a novelist, and the two novels which followed in the early thirties added to his reputation as a leading writer in Norway.

Previously the author had understood man basically in social and political terms. His literary analyses portray man as doomed to a world which acknowledges no absolute center and therefore to an anxious uncertainty. They deal with the problem of the self in its effort to preserve its integrity against social forces, war in particular, which threaten from without.

In the decade of the thirties, however, Fangen began to see a fuller dimension to the problem of the self. A growing emphasis in his writing maintains that man's real dilemma lies in his ignorance of himself. The social realm is almost ignored. Instead, the focus is transferred to the threat to the self from within: irrational forces alienate the self from its own being and from society as well. This shift in emphasis from "without" to "within" is accompanied by a consideration of the Christian doctrine of redemption. Fangen begins to explore the Biblical insight so often stressed by Luther that only God's act in Christ can redeem man from his alienations.

Some Young People describes the "identity crisis" of three University of Oslo students. Nils Bang and Erik Hamre had been friends since childhood, even though their personalities differed: Nils is quiet and reflective, while Erik is an extrovert. Erik's personality, however, cloaks his inferiority feeling in regard to Nils' superior intelligence. Between them stands Astrid, who loves Nils. The relationship of the three young people ends in tragedy when, as a result of a nervous collapse, Nils commits suicide. This event precipitates a religious crisis in Erik's life; he begins to doubt the Christian faith into which he had been nurtured since childhood.

Subsequently he seeks help from his friend, Thoralf Holm, a student of theology. Their long discussions[29] have been singled out as a typical example of the uneasy student attitude toward religion at the time of World War I.[30] In contrast to Erik, Holm values his childhood faith. Yet he is unable to convince Erik that Christian faith is relevant to adult concerns. Erik's indifference to religion grows as he becomes absorbed in a study of law.

Fangen continues the story in the novel Erik. After his climb to success, Erik is nevertheless haunted by a sense of meaninglessness:

> Is there ultimately something outside of space and time, a hope of eternity, a religious hope? So insecure is man's peace that he must place his hope on the other side of life's border. This is the common Christian explanation. And could it well be the right one?[31]

Holm is now able to restore Erik's respect for the Christian religion by an effective discussion of the theology of redemption (pp. 154–162).

Critics identified Erik's religious quest as that of the author while Holm represents the viewpoint of orthodox Lutheranism in dialogue with Fangen.[32] The two novels describe Erik's struggle to orientate his life to a religious dimension in the time of cultural change; although his religious orientation is tentative at the close of the novel, he is inclined to accept Christian faith as an important aspect of his life.

In 1932 the novel <u>Duel</u> (Duell) appeared, and established its author's reputation in the United States. A reviewer for <u>Time</u> magazine wrote:

> When Feodor Dostoevsky died, 53 years ago, a light went out of literature's night sky that appears only once in a blue moon. Last week U.S. readers were rubbing amazed eyes, asking themselves if the moon were not again blue. For <u>Duel</u>, Norwegian author Ronald Fangen's first book to be brought out in the U.S., shone with an unmistakably Dostoevskian light.[33]

<u>Duel</u> elaborates the religious view concerning redemption from sin through divine activity. The physician Klaus Hallem and the professor George Røiter are the principal characters. Their life-long friendship—a "duel"—is described in the novel. The son of wealthy parents, Klaus Hallem is portrayed as neurotic and introspective. In school, he cannot compete successfully with the brilliant George Røiter. In his desperate attempt to do so, he submits a Schopenhauer essay as an original paper. The plagiarism earns him a reprimand before the class. That evening Røiter goes to visit the despairing Hallem and arrives just in time to prevent his suicide.

This incident becomes the axis around which the subsequent lives of the two men are molded. The successful Røiter gives every effort to bolster his country doctor friend's self-respect. But almost any kind of adversity is enough to turn Hallem's mind to self-destruction, and eventually he commits suicide. In the process, Røiter magnifies his own self-respect by contemplating the strengths of his personality: calmness, adjustment, and reason. These strengths are the antithesis of Hallem's weaknesses. But Hallem's death-wish also increases Røiter's fear of death.

At the height of his career, Røiter becomes the innocent victim of a scandal which forces him to resign from his profession. In failing health, and in terror of death, he ponders the selfishness of his friendship with Hallem; he had cultivated it merely in order to have a mirror of his own success. At the end, only religious faith saves Røiter from his anxiety of meaninglessness. On his deathbed he cries, "I thank you, Jesus Christ, for your death in dishonor. I thank you, God, for your grace" (p. 353).

Fangen portrays the leading characters of <u>Some Young People</u>, <u>Erik</u>, and <u>Duel</u> in a similar fashion. The efforts of Nils Bang and Klaus Hallem to overcome spiritual anxiety are climaxed in both instances by suicide. Erik Hamre and George Røiter also suffer from spiritual anxiety, but its effect is different: they are redeemed from it, Erik by his love for Astrid and Røiter by his faith in Christ. Their anxieties give them self-understanding. Fangen repeats this theme in the novel A Woman's Way (En kvinnes vei).[34]

The book that Fangen described as his best novel, The Man Who Loved Righteousness (Mannen som elsket rettferdigheten), was published in November, 1934.[35] The "man" of the novel, shoemaker Gottfried Stein, is obsessed by biblical references to righteousness. As a consequence, he attempts to live as an absolutely righteous person.

When Stein becomes involved in a petty litigation and is unjustly sentenced to serve a day in prison, his passion for righteousness drives him to a frenzied quest for restitution. Every effort he makes, however, is useless. Finally, frustrated and enraged, Stein murders the judge who had sentenced him.

In prison once more, he "felt lost and condemned—by God, by life, and by himself. He wanted to die" (p. 276). As he contemplates his past, he begins to recognize his guilt: he had defended "righteousness" in spite of any consequences to others. His home, for example, had become a terrible place because of his omniscient and selfish bearing. He had ignored love. He begins to understand the biblical insight that no person can establish a right relationship with the holy God upon the basis of his own righteousness. "Yes, I who have never once prayed for love and God's grace," mused Stein, "how could I receive justice and be righteous myself?" (p. 303). Righteousness, he now understands, is a gift from God and not a compensation for human effort. Stein had considered himself as so righteous that he had become unrighteous in his relationship to others, even to the point of murder! In mental and physical anguish, he begins to esteem a different biblical admonition:

> Love...after many years he now understood that it was a command. This was God's law. It both freed and condemned one. Whoever resisted it judged himself...for is not the great commandment this: You shall love? (p. 315).

Drawn together by a common bond of spiritual suffering, Nils Bang, Erik Hallem, George Røiter, and Gottfried Stein are unstable personalities. Ultimately, God sustains Hamre, Røiter, and Stein. For in recognizing the consequences of sin, they are redeemed by divine grace. The content of previous works such as The Weak and A Novel is humanistic; man and the domain of human existence were emphasized. But in Some Young People, Erik, Duel, and The Man Who Loved Righteousness, in which the above characters are depicted, the author's emphasis includes ideas of God and of divine activity. This divine activity is not presented as a miraculous intervention which defies the internal logic of the individuals themselves. Although shaken by traumatic experiences, none of them is struck down by them into believing in God. Rather, through a gradual unfolding of life's experiences the characters perceive that God's workings are not intrusions from the outside, but rather a part of the fuller and richer dimension of their own existence.

During the years from 1929 to 1934 Fangen worked as a journalist for the Oslo daily, Signs of the Times (Tidens tegn). His political commentary also reflected his religious conviction. During a visit to Berlin he became shocked at the upheavals in German politics; in 1932 he voiced his concern that another war might break out in Europe. Nations were "too isolated from each other," he wrote, "and the fact is that Hitler threatens war."[36] He claimed that by their racial policies against the Jews, the Nazis were creating a fantastic new religion, a blending of Christianity with nationalism.

He denounced their racist agitation and wrote that the Church should refrain from any sort of racist religion. Rather, it should free itself to carry its message to all peoples. Fangen expressed his admiration for the German people, despite the excesses of the Third Reich. The government of Germany stood at fault not only because of its racist policy against the Jews, but also because they undertake a blasphemous war against the Christian religion and the German Church...This war in its propagandistic form militates against the religious convictions and consciences of pastors.[38]

In deep awareness of the complexities of the human situation, Fangen endorsed the Christian faith; from it he had taken his views of human responsibility and freedom. His Christian convictions did not cause him to reject the world or, with a false spirituality, to despise it. As he grew in understanding his vocation as a Christian, his Christian convictions had become an ever more powerful factor in his profession as a writer.

2

HØSBJØR
1934–1935

o o o o o o o o o o o o o o o o o o o o o o o o o o o o o o o o o o

"Sing to the Lord, bless his name; tell of his salvation from day to day."

—Psalm 96:2

5
"FRANK"

By 1934 Ronald Fangen, not yet forty years of age, had made notable progress. The failure of the early novels had only bolstered his determination to do better writing, and works such as <u>Fall into Sin</u> and <u>Duel</u> gave a foretaste of more significant literary achievement to come.

But a decisive experience in 1934 brought the promising young author into a new frame of mind, introduced him to a new circle of friends, and eventually left a permanent mark upon his career. It occurred during the fall of the year when he met Frank Buchman and his associates at a large tourist hotel near Hamar called Høsbjør. Here he was brought into contact in a direct way with a new type of American Protestant evangelism known at that time as the Oxford Group Movement.

In order to understand better the decisiveness of this new impulse in Fangen's life it will be necessary to describe the origins of Oxford Group evangelism in the person of its founder, an American Lutheran clergyman known to his many friends as "Frank."

The history of religion in America has often been marked by periods of religious fervor known as "revivals." Since the "Great Awakening" of the eighteenth century, revivalism has been established as a permanent feature of American Protestantism. In the past, revivalism has been associated with the names of Dwight L. Moody and Billy Sunday. Today it is linked with the name of Billy Graham.

For the most part, revivals have touched people in the middle and lower classes of society and lifted many of them to higher standards of morality. One revival has been unusual, however, in that it has touched people of the upper classes, both in America and Europe. Led by Frank N.D. Buchman, and first known as the "First Century Christian Fellowship" and later as the "Oxford Group Movement," this revival began in the 1920's and is active today under the name "Moral Re-Armament" (MRA). From international headquarters in Caux, Switzerland and Mackinac Island, Michigan, MRA seeks to promote its cause through personal appeals and by means of dramas, movies, and full-page newspaper advertisements.[1]

Frank Nathan Daniel Buchman was born on June 4, 1878, in modest circumstances, in the town of Pennsburg, Pennsylvania. In his youth he showed no special qualities of mind or spirit. Yet by the time he died, aged eighty-three, in 1961, the movement he had created was internationally recognized and "he had been photographed with and decorated by more monarchs, statesmen, and other potentates than any other religious leader, except, possibly the Pope."[2] Pennsburg lies in the heart of the "Pennsylvania-Dutch" country; Buchman's forefathers had migrated to Pennsylvania from a German-speaking section of Switzerland and throughout his life he showed a special affection for Germany, for his native Pennsylvania, and for Allentown, to which his parents moved when he was fifteen. From the deeply religious German Lutheran background of his parents, Buchman received the formative influences upon his own inner life. One important influence was the Pennsylvania Lutheran pietism which nourished Buchman's religious development.

Walter H. Clark has described this pietism, which he maintains is still alive in the small towns of modern Pennsylvania.[3] It dates from the latter half of the seventeenth century and the work of Philip Jacob Spener (d. 1705), who championed Luther's doctrine of the universal priesthood of believers. Spener advocated that more recognition be given to the rights of the individual Christian as over against those of the clergy, and he favored more responsibility for control of the church being placed in the hands of the congregations. He further emphasized the study of the Scriptures by the laity and meetings for Bible-reading and mutual edification in Christian living. To Spener, personal piety was more important than doctrinal soundness and the practical nature of Christianity made conduct a matter of greater importance than knowledge. As Pietism developed, Spener advocated character transformation and moral perfection as a goal for Christians.[4] Through the efforts of such men as Nicholaus Zinzendorf and Henry Muhlenberg, both followers of the Pietist tradition from the University of Halle, Pietism became a foundation of colonial Lutheranism, particularly in Pennsylvania: "The most able Lutheran pastors in colonial America were Pietists...and a mild type of Pietism was a continuing influence among the colonial Lutherans."[5] Clark traces a parallel emphasis between the religious views of Pietism described above and the views Buchman promoted in the Oxford Group Movement, namely, the universal priesthood of believers, meetings for Christian edification, and the insistence upon moral perfection.[6]

Buchman graduated from the Allentown High School and entered Muhlenberg College, from which he received an A.B. degree in 1899. He then entered the Mt. Airy Lutheran Theological Seminary, in Philadelphia, from which he was graduated in 1902. During these years he was exposed to a theologically conservative atmosphere. The faculty at Mt. Airy Seminary was at that time orientated to a conservatism which had little sympathy with current biblical criticism, dismissing it as an "attack upon the Bible"; its teaching was calculated to demonstrate the superiority of seventeenth century Lutheran orthodoxy to other religious views.[7] For the rest of his life Buchman remained a theological conservative and was indifferent to biblical criticism and new currents of theological thinking.

From 1902 to 1905, Buchman served as the pastor of the Church of the Good Shepherd, Overbrook, Pennsylvania. In addition to his pastoral duties, he organized the first Luther Hospice in America at Overbrook in 1904. He also founded a home for boys, the Luther Settlement House, in Philadelphia, in 1905. The Philadelphia venture was so successful that from this enterprise other settlement houses were founded. Soon Buchman gave up his congregational work entirely and devoted himself to them. During this period he also spent some time in the homes of the wealthy, presumably to enlist financial support for his projects. In his work at the Philadelphia settlement house, he is reported to have converted many boys to the Christian religion, but in 1908 he fell into sharp disagreement with the trustees over a matter of policy and, in anger, resigned.[8]

He sought escape from this bitter experience in a trip to Europe. While in England and worshipping in a tiny village church at Keswick, Buchman had an experience of decisive importance in bringing about the Oxford Group Movement. There the tired and discouraged American pastor listened to a woman speaker deliver a simple, conversational talk about the Cross of Christ to a gathering of about seventeen persons. Buchman described his reaction:

> A doctrine which I knew as a boy, which my church believed, which I had always been taught and which that day became a great reality for…a wave of strong emotion, following the will to surrender, rose up within me from the depths of an estranged spiritual life, and seemed to lift my soul from its anchorage of selfishness…to the foot of the Cross.[9]

The day afterward, he wrote to Philadelphia and asked forgiveness from the people whom he felt had opposed his humanitarian aims: "I have nursed ill will against you. I am sorry. Forgive me? Sincerely, Frank." He received no replies to his letters, but from that time on he began to feel a new power and gladness in his inner life.[10]

Returning to the United States in 1908, he was appointed secretary of the Y.M.C.A. at Pennsylvania State College. Here his principles and methods of personal evangelism were given their first test. From 1909 until the spring of 1915, he remained at Pennsylvania State, experimenting in evangelism and developing his ideas. He succeeded in attracting to his program an increasing proportion of the students, particularly to his voluntary Bible studies. Two visits to the Orient during the years 1916–1919 acquainted him with the missionary enterprise, and especially with the personal inner struggles of individual missionaries, to whom he gave special attention.[11]

His next position was that of extension lecturer in "Personal Evangelism" at Hartford Seminary, First appointed in the spring of 1916, he lived at Hosmer Hall, a student dormitory, for two years; his appointment, which allowed him to take long leaves of absence, was renewed annually until his withdrawal in 1922. At Hartford he conducted an early morning prayer group which some of the students regularly attended, but his efforts there were not as successful as those at Pennsylvania State; some students complained that he interrupted their studies and faculty members opposed him because of his criticism of their lack of evangelical fervor. Once more Buchman became discouraged, feeling hampered by his colleagues and authorities at Hartford. He felt a need for freedom and that his mission was to "convert the world." Consequently, in December, 1921, while on his way to Washington, D.C., to attend the World Disarmament Conference, he made a decision: he would give up his job and risk all his energies in the cause of world revival. According to Walter Clark, this decision launched Buchman on his unique career and marks the beginning of the Group Movement.[12]

In 1918 Buchman's work in China had begun to attract attention. Here the first "houseparty" was held at Kuling, a resort in central China. At this time he acquired two effective disciples: Sherwood S. Day, a Yale graduate and Hartford student, and the Reverend Samuel Shoemaker, Jr., a Princeton graduate and at that time engaged in missionary work in China. These two men became the nucleus for Buchman's campaigns in eastern colleges during the next several years. In the summer of 1921 Buchman made a convert at Oxford, Loudon Hamilton, who joined the work in the United States. Describing his work as a "Christian revolution," Buchman portrayed his Movement as a

> Christian revolution whose concern is vital Christianity. Its aim is a new social order under the dictatorship of the Spirit of God, making for better relationships, for unselfish co-operation, for cleaner business, cleaner politics, for the elimination of political, industrial and racial antagonisms...World-changing will come through life-changing. To bring about this new order the Oxford Group believes that a world-wide spiritual awakening is the only hope.[13]

From 1921–1924, Buchman's efforts in American universities achieved a remarkable success. During the summer holidays, Oxford and Cambridge became centers of Group activity. International visitations by teams of youthful converts were begun and "Buchmanism" was widely discussed on both sides of the Atlantic. Van Dusen reports that

> Something approaching revival began to stir the campuses of Princeton, Yale, Harvard, Williams, Smith, Vassar, Bryn Mawr—the most unlikely colleges in the land. Men flocked into the leadership of the church. Of the fifty ablest ministers on the Atlantic seaboard today, somewhere near half were directed into their vocation through his influence at that time.[14]

At Oxford and Cambridge universities, the Movement had modest headway, making an appeal in particular to the religiously-minded athlete. Rejecting both the large mass-meeting and the college religious conference methods of evangelism, Buchman turned to a more subtle method, the religious "houseparty." Collegians were invited not to conferences or prayer meetings or revivals but to small and informal meetings, often in the homes of wealthy people Buchman relied upon for support. Primarily, the houseparty was a device for bringing together in an atmosphere of friendly informality members of the Movement and prospective converts in order to introduce the latter to the "spirit" and "way of life" of the Buchmanites. Houseparties ranging in size from twenty to a hundred and fifty participants were held both in England and in America.[15]

One participant described a houseparty he attended as a "spiritual clinic" and wrote

> We gathered—Harvard undergraduates and graduate students; Worcester businessmen, a professor of theology, and a freshman from Bowdoin—crowding in circles about the fireplace. Until eleven we sat there, while a few of the leaders spoke informally of the purpose of the party, and each member of the group briefly introduced himself...the group was entertained by stories of the various members, but they were discussing religion...That was the miracle: no feeling of something uncanny, no pious solemnity, but perfect naturalness.[16]

By 1924 criticism of Buchman and his followers began to mount. The officers of Princeton University, moved by criticisms that the Movement had pried into personal matters of sex and that it was dangerous from a psychological viewpoint, conducted an investigation and requested Buchman not to return to the campus. Soon afterward his followers there withdrew. Opposition was also aroused at Harvard and Yale, and many of the early adherents fell away or turned to more usual types of religious effort.[17]

Disappointed but undismayed, Buchman shifted his base of operation to England. Loudon Hamilton returned to Oxford for full-time work in the university in the fall of 1925. Julian Thornton-Duesbury, a chaplain at Wycliffe Hall, became actively associated with Hamilton's efforts; gradually, small groups of undergraduates began to meet together for meditation at the beginning of each day. Beginning in the fall of 1926, open meetings for witness were held on Sunday evenings. By now Buchman placed stronger emphasis upon the discipline of his followers and gave careful attention to the training of leaders. During 1927 weekly meetings of an "inner" group of leaders were held, and the years from 1925 to 1927 provided time for a valuable consolidation of the Movement.[18]

In 1928, "teams" of trained and disciplined workers began to cross the ocean to America, to South America and to the Orient. The names "First Century Christian Fellowship" and "Buchmanism" had been used to describe the movement since 1921. The new name, "Oxford Group," originated in South Africa: a railway porter is said to have scribbled the phrase on labels stuck on the windows of the reserved compartments in which a team of Buchmanites from Oxford were traveling and the South African press picked up the phrase.[19] The "Oxford Group" described Buchman's religious movement until 1938, when he inaugurated its new title, "Moral Re-Armament."

6
LIFE CHANGERS

"World-changing will come through life-changing," Buchman proclaimed. "Apart from changed lives no civilization can endure."[20] Oxford Group literature is filled with dramatic examples of its success, especially among professional people and college students. Much of the early progress of the Movement did indeed rest upon "changed" lives and the testimonies of converts were used in a powerful way to persuade others to "change." One Group pamphlet lists several assumptions and interpretations which defined its position concerning the changed life. One was that "men are sinners." Constant reference was made by Groupers to "secret" sins; those who had been "changed" had made an "absolute" break with sin and been delivered from the spiritual twilight of ordinary Christian experience. Maintaining that moral difficulties always lay behind intellectual problems, the Group asserted that if moral obstacles (usually related to sex and the use of money) were removed, intellectual difficulties would dissolve.[21] Hence, the Group emphasized the need for an essentially moral conversion to new standards of personal conduct. Buchman listed four "absolute" standards:

> Absolute honesty, absolute purity, absolute unselfishness, absolute love. Those are Christ's standards. Are they yours? You may have to put things straight. I had to. I began by writing six people, admitting that ill will between us was my fault, and not theirs. Remember—if you want the world to get straight, get straight yourself.[22]

The "Four Absolutes" were held to be a standard against which an individual might measure his failure to realize God's perfect ideal for his life, as epitomized by Christ's life and character. Genuine Christian conversion was marked by a voluntary surrender of one's total life to this standard. The original source for this standard of morality appeared to be Christ's Sermon on the Mount.

The American, V.C. Kitchen, testified that the change he experienced at a New York houseparty was sudden and sharp; by presenting a moral challenge, instead of a demand for "faith," the Group transformed his life in a manner "parallel to the life of early Christians." First, however, Kitchen had had to confess his sins before God and men.[23] The self-revelations of dishonesty and impurity which became common at houseparties left the Group open to the charge of being morbidly interested in such matters.

When nominal Christians became "changed," a serious tension between the Group and orthodox churches often developed. Two effective apologists for the Group in this regard were Emil Brunner and Samuel Shoemaker.[24] In his scholarly approach, Brunner attempted to harmonize the efforts of both the Group and the orthodox churches by declaring that in the face of increased secularization of society the Church's missionary task had become blunted and the Group had responded to this crisis:

> In the Group Movement there has been set before our eyes once again the primitive Christian experience, that the Christians can be actually a salt of the earth and a light of the world…Renewal of the bond of marriage, renewal of family relations, of master and servant, even a renewal of whole communities has been set before our eyes as an accomplished fact.[25]

According to Shoemaker, "the Group seeks to serve the Church from within…it has no other organization than the Church, no formal membership of its own, and is wholly identified with the Christian Church."[26] Buchman's followers appeared to be more concerned about the development of a company of "truly enlightened" within the Church than about any form of ecclesiastical organization or emphasis.

"Guidance" is another Group emphasis which related to the idea that God has a "plan" for each human life. Group literature gives no precise definition of the subject, and the practice of receiving God's guidance as a result of an individual's "quiet time" became a controversial issue. According to Buchman

> The Holy Spirit is the most intelligent source of information in the world today. He has the answer to every problem. Everywhere when men will let Him, He is teaching them how to live.[27]

Biblical references (Acts 8:36; 9:11; 10:11–20, and Rom. 8:14) were cited as examples of "guidance" taken from the New Testament. One Oxford sympathizer claims that the truth of divine guidance has always been an historic doctrine of the Church and that the Oxford Group had worked for its rediscovery "by the ordinary man and the statesman."[28]

Buchman envisioned a "quiet time with the Holy Spirit," early in the morning before the daily round of activities began, as a moment when God could impress His counsel. He suggested that a pencil and notebook be used to record "God-given thoughts and ideas" so that no detail, however small, could be lost. Guidance was then to be "checked" according to the teaching of the Bible or by conferences with other Groupers. Prayer was also to be a part of the "quiet time" which appeared to supplant attendance at orthodox Christian worship services for many Groupers.[29]

Common examples of what the Group termed "guidance" concerned decisions regarding the spending of money, travel plans, and ways to approach prospective converts. A.J. Russell testified that his book, For Sinners Only, which helped spread the Movement in the nineteen thirties, was written as a result of guidance.[30] In Group practice guidance was given a more prominent position than reason as a method for ordering life. Whereas orthodox churches committed themselves to an often unspectacular and painstaking task of gradual spiritual upbuilding through a process of Christian education and nurture, the Group stressed the necessity of immediate, observable results of Christian faith. This led not only to a misleading emphasis but also to guidance which was often trivial, such as the boy who was guided to eat his breakfast food and the woman who was guided in the selection of new lighting fixtures for her home. Buchman was not immune from this danger to "absolute honesty." Henry Van Dusen writes:

> In the course of a day I have heard Mr. Buchman report twenty or twenty-five instances of direct guidance...Perhaps a fourth or a fifth of them actually came to pass. They were triumphantly cited as vindications of the practice. The great bulk which at the end of the day remained unfulfilled were blithely ignored.[31]

Sherwood Day insisted, however, that all of the principles of the Group were principles of the Bible; guidance had been the experience of Samuel, Isaiah, Jonah, and Paul: "Guidance is simply the experience of God flooding into a man's life, to give him direction and power." The Group, then, was "a way of life, not an organization, not a sect, not even a new method."[32] In seeking to remain interdenominational and free from doctrinal statements, the Movement conceived itself to be a way of life and a force to revitalize the orthodox churches.

"Sharing" involved the practice of confessing moral failures to one another. As with guidance this experience had a Biblical foundation (I John 1:3) and it became a familiar feature of houseparties as well as between friends in the Group. In sharing one made known to others his personal failures and defeats and, at the same time, of the help received through contact with comrades in the Group. Even at the cost of personal humiliation, Groupers insisted that this procedure was necessary to genuine Christian experience because the primary appeal of the Movement was to the will and not to the intellect: "what is wrong with the world individually, socially, nationally, and racially is purely moral corruption and not mere intellectual misconception."[33] The "life changers" insisted that personal moral failure needed to be brought "into the open" and dealt with.

Harold Begbie, one of Buchman's early disciples in England, wrote of the value of sharing with Buchman, the "soul surgeon," whose manner of hearing confession differed from that practiced in orthodox churches; he required those who confessed their sins, whatever their profession in life, to go out and "save other souls."[34] Because the liturgies of the various representatives of historic Christendom often needed the understanding of long custom, the Group had reached people with the Gospel for whom conventional Christianity had little meaning. Its simple but powerful witness for Christ had accomplished what the organized Churches had in many instances failed to do.

However, the nature of some of the public sharing sessions staged in the earlier stages of the Group's development brought criticism upon it. Some had felt impelled to confess their sexual sins; some of these uninhibited confessions were shocking to outsiders, and led them to believe that there was an unhealthy sex emphasis in the movement. Efforts were made to correct this tendency, but sharing continued as an essential feature of the Movement. More orthodox Christians complained that as the "changed life" concept ignored the Christian sacrament of Baptism, so the method for continuing the changed life, "sharing," ignored the Christian sacrament of the Lord's Supper.

The theological foundations of the Group Movement described above supported its attempt to force potential converts to face the facts of their personal lives in a courageous manner. If an individual did this in the prescribed Group manner of confession and sharing, he was then given a definite rationale for undertaking new habits of life. Although no statistics are available, the Group provided power for many people to re-direct their lives by its challenge to absolute consecration. At the same time, however, this challenge to consecration fostered a spiritual pride which oversimplified religious issues and life's problems (Groupers were fond of saying, "There are only two classes of people: the changed and the unchanged.") Moralism tended to be substituted for the traditional worship of God and it overestimated human experiences in comparison with the Bible's emphasis upon the acts of God, and traditional theology's stress upon the concept of divine revelation. In addition to its neglect of theology, the Oxford Group could not escape the criticism of social snobbery and exaggerated reports of success. Some observers have defended the Group as a needed reminder to orthodox churches of the continued necessities of genuine fellowship among church members and of their obligation to win converts. The distinguished church historian Kenneth Latourette has suggested that because the Oxford

Group was a twentieth century movement which worked with some success for the revitalization of existing structures within the Church, it provides an example of the vitality of the Christian religion in modern times.[35]

At the invitation of Carl Hambro, President of the Norwegian Parliament, Buchman prepared a "team" of thirty followers to accompany him to Norway.[36] When they arrived there in 1934 Ronald Fangen's "change" was one of the spectacular successes of the movement in Europe.

7
OXFORD GROUP DYNAMICS

The work of the Group in Norway got under way when approximately one hundred leading citizens of Norway—politicians, writers, Churchmen, labor leaders and industrialists—came to Høsbjør, a large tourist hotel near Hamar, to meet Buchman and the thirty team members.[37] At the suggestion of the head-master and former seminary dean in China, Sten Bugge, Fangen's name was included on the invitation list.[38]

The meeting, which began on October 27 and continued until November 4, received wide coverage in the Oslo press. Among the Churchmen in attendance were the Bishop of Haalogaland, Eivind Berggrav, and the noted professor of Old Testament at the University of Oslo, Sigmund Mowinckel. One of the leaders of the "team," besides Buchman, was Loudon Hamilton. On November 4, when the houseparty concluded its programs, almost a thousand Norwegians had vis-ited Group sessions at the hotel.[39]

The houseparty promoted no formal agenda but was skill-fully managed. Buchman, Hamilton and other team members "shared" and gained the attention of their listeners. One visitor was impressed by the total absence of religious cere-mony; on occasion, he reported, the gathering divided into three groups: women, clergymen and laymen. At these meetings in smaller rooms of the hotel, silent prayer was encouraged and short introductory speeches promoted sharing from Group members. Bible studies were an important activity; Bishop Berggrav recalled the sight of Fangen at a study led by Buchman: "he sat in the front row of chairs, holding his head in his hands, deeply impressed by what he heard."[40]

Fangen had arrived at Høsbjør with a cynical attitude about the Group; to guard against boredom, he brought along several books he had been assigned to review, plus several bottles of liquor. But he had no time either for the books or the liquor, because at one of the sessions he was "changed." An observer described Fangen's response: "The most moving moment of the session," he wrote, "occurred when the well-known author Ronald Fangen arose and gave himself to God, It happened quietly, and with dignity, without sensation."[41] Another observer reported that Fangen was especially impressed by Loudon Hamilton's sharing; he recalled the words Fangen used in his first public response to the team: "I stand before you as a free man, and I have confidence in you people."[42]

What impressed him about the houseparty, he wrote afterwards, was that the team had demonstrated a Christian comradeship and a fresh approach to Christian morality. The members' varying social and national backgrounds had been made subordinate to their decision to live a Christian life. Their genuineness and spontaneity appealed to him because he had long wished for an ability to live a similar kind of compromise-free Christian life: he believed that "life-changing" had indeed occurred at Høsbjør. "To the Oxford team, none named, none forgotten," he wrote, "my gratitude shall always remain."[43]

Years later Buchman recalled the houseparty's affect upon Fangen:

> I remember those days in Høsbjør most vividly and the impact of Fredrik Ramm and Ronald Fangen which then spilled over the whole country, and then to Denmark and later to Sweden.[44]

Another person similarly impressed with the houseparty was a lawyer, Erling Wikborg. He related that the members of the team shared their small, personal dishonesties so earnestly that in each witness one could see a mirror of himself. Guests were invited to share their personal failures with team representatives. Fangen and Wikborg decided to share with a team member from South America. In this process, Wikborg said, they discovered simple truths of Christianity: selfishness (sin), one's inadequacy in dealing with sin (need), and the answer (Christ). According to Wikborg, sharing in this manner gave one a psychological release, and a new freedom; having a "happier" Christianity made one eager to spread it.[45]

"Fangen is converted. And will convert his friends!" was the newspaper report in The Daily News (Dagbladet) of Fangen's participation at the houseparty. His response to the Group was described as follows:

> Finally, I had to admit I had lived a dishonest life. I acknowledged my sin and received God's forgiveness. It was the happiest day of my life. Even though I do not like the word 'conversion,' I must now turn and forsake my old life. But I will not forsake my old friends, for I will win them. All my life I have thought as a Christian and had Christian ideas, but I did not want to live as a Christian. My reasoning was that Christianity's moral claims were relative, valid only for the time in which they were written. Thus I tried to explain away Christianity's absolute claim...I will continue to write. But now I will write for this cause in which I believe, and will seek to win my friends for it.[46]

The activities at Høsbjør were reported by other Oslo newspapers also. The Worker's News (Arbeiderbladet) was skeptical of the Group's apparent preference for "high class" society, and also for what it termed its naiveté: "Do Fangen or Hambro believe that on some fine day Hitler will greet a Jew and ask for forgiveness?"[47] The conservative newspaper, The Evening News (Aftenposten), was generally sympathetic to the Group and its Høsbjør houseparty, but the writer, Helge Krog, scoffed at the goings-on in the liberal Daily News:

> The new luxury Christianity at Høsbjør has won two: Fredrik Ramm and Ronald Fangen...It is noteworthy that Fangen will not only think as a Christian but also live as one.[48]

Aware of this skepticism, Fangen defended the Group in an article in Signs of the Times entitled, "A Christian World Revolution: Concerning the Oxford Group and the meeting at Høsbjør." "Buchman, he wrote, "has a gifted way of understanding people and is not interested in personal reward." Sharing was not exhibitionism, he maintained, but rather a means of promoting the "Communion of saints," a basic Lutheran theological foundation.[49] He had discovered that Buchman did not ask one to speculate about the mysteries of the Christian religion; rather, one was asked to relate episodes from his experiences in Christian living. The Oxford Group called for an unqualified surrender of an individual's will in order to achieve compromise-free Christian living. After changing the individual in this manner, the Group then reached out "into the world." Its gospel was a simple one: vital faith, experienced religion, and the dictatorship of the Spirit. "I am convinced, he wrote, "that the Oxford Group is the greatest spiritual power of our time. We experience again the times of the apostles...."[50]

One of Fangen's friends from the days of his editorship of Our World, Henrik Groth, expressed his view of the author's experience at Høsbjør by saying, "He was really conquered by the people he met there. He changed totally and freed himself from the danger of alcoholism." The decisive significance of the Høsbjør houseparty has also been affirmed by Solveig Fangen.[51] Not only had the meeting given Fangen a new religious orientation; it also resulted in new friendships Fangen made with people who were impressed in a similar manner as he had been: Erling Wikborg, a journalist, Fredrik Ramm, and a physician, Einar Lundby.

8
CAMPAIGNING IN NORWAY

When the Høsbjør houseparty adjourned on November 4, the team, supported now by Norwegian converts, came to Oslo to continue the "campaign." Buchman and Fangen, together with two professors of theology at the University of Oslo, Sigmund Mowinkel and Lyder Brun, participated in a meeting at the Blindern student dormitories of the University. Led by Loudon Hamilton, the meeting publicized the Group's arrival in Norway. Fangen addressed the students and emphasized that he would no longer remain a nominal Christian.

On November 9, Hamilton announced a public gathering would be held at the Logens Meeting Hall in downtown Oslo; this procedure was unusual in Group practice, he mentioned, because the Group usually preferred to operate at private gatherings. The meeting which followed several days afterward drew a capacity audience. Hamilton and other foreign members of the team addressed the assembly. Fangen and another Norwegian convert, Fredrik Ramm, also spoke in praise of the Group and its aims. Buchman, however, stated that he was not satisfied with the attempt to work with such large numbers of people.[52]

Thus far in its work in Norway, the Group had drawn no distinction between clergy and laity in making its appeal. Pastors were approached by team members in the same manner in which lay people were approached; they, too, were asked to confess their sins, to make restitution, and to follow the "Four Absolutes." One pastor, who had had contact with the Group in its early efforts in Norway, related that this practice made a strong and positive impression upon some clergymen.

One of the clergy participants in the Høsbjør houseparty organized a Group meeting for pastors in Oslo. Approximately three hundred attended and heard Buchman announce his program; all of his knowledge of theology, he said, had not made him a "fisher of men." Thereupon he asked his audience, "Are you life changers?"[53] The Group appeared to have met certain spiritual needs in the lives of the pastors it dealt with, and it helped create a new atmosphere more open to Christian dialogue. It had alerted both clergy and laity to the apparent success of forthright evangelism.

Another large public gathering was sponsored by the Group at the Calmeyer Street Mission House in Oslo. Four thousand persons heard John Watt, a clergyman from Edinburgh, and Reginald Holme, a student from Oxford, share their enthusiasm for the new habits of living they had learned from Buchman. The final speaker was Buchman himself. He emphasized the importance of personal prayer and closed the meeting with a "quiet time." The day following, Buchman led prominent Group members on a visit to the Viking Ship Museum in Oslo. He referred to his followers as "modern Vikings," numbering one million people throughout the world, who were out to "win mankind to the idea of true humanity."[54]

The Oxford Group campaign in Norway was enhanced during the closing weeks of 1934 by the newspaper articles of its respected Norwegian spokesmen such as Sigmund Mowinckel. He pointed out that the Group and the Church of Norway shared similar traditions. The Group had merely used up-to-date language to express traditional Church beliefs. It proclaimed conversion, he maintained, in the same manner that the writers of the New Testament did. The "Four Absolutes" pointed the way to a program of spiritual self-examination which could benefit every Christian. Mowinckel reminded his readers that the Old Testament "Psalms of Thanksgiving" stressed the importance of a believer's witnessing to his salvation; writings of the prophets underscored the fact of God's "leading" human life and of God's speaking to men, he declared. The Group's intention was not to create any new sect; rather, it sought to awaken Christians in all denominations to a more vital Christian life. Thus, Mowinckel concluded, it had built "surprising bridges over confessional, organizational, and historical divisions in the Church."[55]

"The houseparty at Høsbjør," wrote one observer, "was an absolute success." He added that "the religious gatherings in Oslo which had resulted from it were the largest in many years."[56] By 1935 it had become somewhat of a vogue for Norwegians to attend fashionable Oslo houseparties where they could meet members of an international team of Buchmanites.

From Oslo the religious movement spread to other parts of Norway. A second houseparty, led by Buchman and Hamilton, was staged at the resort center of Geilo, northwest of Oslo on the Oslo-Bergen railway. Among the one hundred participants were students, pastors, lawyers, teachers, and businessmen who had come to Geilo from Oslo, Drammen, Fredrikstad, Skien and Bergen.[57]

The Group's activity aroused intense interest in Bergen during December 1935. Overflow crowds attended church services where Fangen was a leading Group spokesman. Outside one church building, Fredrik Ramm presented the challenges of "life-changing" to those who had been unable to gain entrance. Ramm, Fangen, and Carl J. Hambro also assisted Buchman at a meeting in Bergen's Logens Meeting Hall. During the campaign in Bergen, it was estimated that ten thousand citizens of the city had come into contact with the Groupers.

Meanwhile, another team had moved northward to Trondheim. Catherine Hambro, Elise Herschein, and Erling Wikborg were members of this team which enjoyed a similar response to its efforts.[58]

During the spring months of 1935, Fangen began to travel in the other Scandinavian countries on behalf of the Group. In March, he spoke in Engelbrecht's Church in Stockholm, and also appeared with Buchman in Copenhagen. In. May, he addressed a gathering in St. John's Church in Helsinki.

Back in Norway, he related to a group of teachers at Knattholmen his memory of the Høsbjør experience:

> I had the great experience of living in God's power in a way I had never dreamed about. It resulted in a totally new life. I understood that it was not enough for one to pray for the coming of God's kingdom; one must also work for it.

Following his sermon at the Larvik Church, a newspaper reported that "it was a great experience for the congregation to hear his speech, carried by a deep faith and positive relationship to fundamental Christian teachings."[59]

From Larvik Fangen left for Oslo to speak at the University. In this address he emphasized Christianity as a universal religion, and paid tribute to the Swedish clergyman, Nathan Soderblom, for his contribution to the cause of Christian unity. In her report of the convocation Barbra Ring stated that interest in Fangen's appearance had been so high that the University Assembly Hall was filled long before the opening time.[60]

In the far north," Sten Bugge led a team to Tromsø. Eivind Berggrav, at that time head of the Haalogaland bishopric, helped arrange the team's schedule. Before a crowded assembly in the Cathedral Church, Sigmund Mowinckel introduced the Oxford Group team by saying

> This is no new Christianity, no organization or sect. We are only Christians who have been changed and are glad. With the way the world is now, people must become different. And it is you and I who shall make this difference.

Testimonials from teachers, pastors, physicians, businessmen, housewives, and students followed Mowinckel's speech. All related how their lives had become enriched through contacts with the Oxford Group. After having campaigned in Tromsø from August 22 until September 2, the team moved on to Bodø.[61]

Fangen's book, <u>A Christian World Revolution</u> (<u>En kristen verdensrevolution</u>), appeared in 1935. Bearing the subtitle, "My Meeting with the Oxford Group Movement," it contains a description of the Høsbjør houseparty as well as a survey of Group methods of evangelism. After describing his "change," Fangen foresaw the Group as a forerunner of a Christian "world revolution":

> From many corners of the world it is evident that social conditions and the entire human atmosphere have been changed by the Groups' work...We in Norway have also been able to see something in our midst. Great things happen each day. And we are only at the beginning. This revolutionary Christian world movement is steadily at work in many parts of the world. The international team enters a country and leaves, but behind it are left living groups to carry on the work.

His enthusiastic response to the Group, and his efforts on behalf of its cause led one writer to name him the "Oxford Group's Norwegian leader."[62]

In a tribute he paid to Fredrik Ramm in 1946, Fangen attested that the Høsbjør houseparty had brought both of them "into a crisis which was decisive for our lives."[63] The crisis had not only gained new friends for the author such as Fredrik Ramm. It also changed his professional activity and brought him into the thick of the controversy which followed the Oxford Group's campaign in Norway.

3

FERMENT IN THE CHURCH 1935–1940

○ ○

"This is the day which the Lord has made; let us rejoice and be glad in it."

—Psalm 118:24

9
CHRISTIAN REVOLUTIONARY

A common tendency of religious movements such as Moral Re-Armament is that they separate themselves from the more orthodox church bodies. Fangen's involvement with Buchman's followers, however, resulted in an opposite tendency: instead of withdrawing from the Church of Norway, he was stimulated to participate more actively in its affairs. With the passion of one who had experienced the New Testament's description of the word of God as "living and active, sharper than any two-edged sword, piercing to the division of soul and spirit...discerning the thoughts and intentions of the heart," he urged his Church on toward what he conceived to be a "revolutionary" participation in men's lives.[1]

Since the recent appearance of two now famous books, John A.T. Robinson's Honest to God and Harvey Cox's The Secular City, the word "secular" has become a familiar term in contemporary theological debate. In contrast to previous suspicions of everything "merely human" in our world, many theologians now recognize and appreciate the claims and achievements of the secular world. There is general agreement that the outlook of our time has become increasingly this-worldly, or secular, and that the Church must come to grips with this fact, both in its proclamation and its practice of the Christian faith.

All agree that the present outlook is in a state of flux and rapid change. And by participating in this circumstance the Christian faces a dilemma: on the one hand, he may welcome the secularization of our times by urging the church to give up judgmental attitudes in order to adjust, if possible, to the secular mentality; on the other hand, he may adopt a more critical view of secular achievement and insist that Christian faith provides the criterion by which the methods and goals of secular civilization are to be measured. In his book A Christian World Revolution Fangen adopts the latter posture. Here he defends the methods of the Oxford Group as genuinely Christian and proclaims it as "revolutionary Christian movement" which had already taken a long step toward making a worldwide impact. The Høsbjør convert was lavish in his praise:

> From many parts of the world there is evidence that social circumstances and the whole atmosphere of human relationships have been altered on account of the Oxford Group's efforts (p. 116).

Among Fangen's friends and colleagues in Norway were those, however, who were skeptical about this new "revolutionary" stance. Alf Larsen wrote a stinging criticism of Buchman's disciples in the periodical Janus. He describes the "changed" as having only materialistic concern for Christianity; the Group merely pretends to be disinterested in financial matters, he maintains; it was actually well organized in this area. Larsen contrasts the theo-centricity of Barth and Kierkegaard with what he terms the Group's "subjective" idea of guidance. He warns that the Group encourages self-illusion by its emphasis upon success, and that guidance could not be substituted for serious theological discussion. In his opinion, the Group was in reality "a denial of all religion."[2]

Negative reactions to the Group also came from those who were not professionally related to the Church of Norway. In his review of A Christian World Revolution, Einar Skavlan asserts that Fangen, in a naive manner, had wrongly assumed that his religious experience was applicable to Norway and the entire world. He reminds his readers that other religions besides Christianity had taught high moral principles. Ingjald Nissen complains that Fangen's book downgrades man's powers of reason. Christian Smit was also disappointed with Fangen's "Oxford" book because he believed the author had become too susceptible to the "Buchman jargon." Smit called upon Fangen to stand, as he had done in the past, as a "revolutionary individualist."[3] The author Helge Krog wrote a description of Group activity in 1938 and characterizes it as a "Christian masquerade;" but he maintained that Fangen had aided its progress in Norway by making such extravagant claims about its success.[4]

In a more positive response to the Movement, Sverre Norberg compares its work in Norway to the accomplishments of Hans Nielsen Hauge because both emphasized "complete surrender" to Christ and recognized the reality of sin. Norberg believes Hauge would have endorsed the Group's work and climaxes his survey when he writes, "It is a time of grace to be allowed to live in the time of Karl Barth and the Oxford Group Movement."[5] In Sigurd Norman's analysis of the Group he called attention to Luther's own intensely personal religious experience. "The essential importance of the Group for Norway's Christians," he concluded, "is that they put into practice the values of life already in their possession."[6] Representatives of Norway's Inner Mission Society discussed the Group at their general convention in Oslo on July 1, 1935. The secretary, Johannes M. Wisløff, declared before this convention of conservative Christians that

Oxford goes in the direction of freeing itself from doctrine. We notice that it does not clearly raise the banner of Christ's atonement. As far as the struggle with liberal theology is concerned, we notice that the Group has not definitely separated itself from it.

Ole Hallesby agreed with the secretary, and, according to a report of the meeting, stated that from the viewpoint of conservative Christians, the Group Movement proclaimed "a Gospel without the Cross."[7]

For several years following the Group campaign in Norway the pros and cons of its activity continued to be discussed in Church periodicals and books. The existence of this literature suggests that the Movement had instigated a religious revival of sorts among some of the members of the State Church of Norway. However, the national impact of the Oxford Group Movement in Norway is difficult to describe apart from considering its effect on the lives of individuals such as Fangen. One broad reaction to its program of evangelism was an increase in the frankness with which Norwegians spoke about Christian concerns. Among the clergy, the "cure of souls" became a widespread activity, and their counseling efforts strengthened the work of the Church in a neglected area.[8]

Another reaction was the renewed awareness of Church ecumenicity which Buchman and his international team had given to Norwegian Christians. Buchman challenged his Olso listeners in March, 1935, to increase this awareness:

You have only begun. Five months? Five years? Every person changed? Every business? Whole cities getting direction? Politics? A nation listening to God? International relationships?...I believe that Norway will take this message to other countries.[9]

In A Christian World Revolution Fangen gave his positive and optimistic response to Buchman's persuasive call.

His next "Oxford" book, The New Life (Det nye liv), contains speeches the author gave before student groups and congregations during 1935. The Church, Fangen insists, had too often "withdrawn from the world" and its goals had become obscure; it would be all right for the Church to gather its members for periodic "withdrawals," but only for the purpose of equipping them to penetrate secular life with its gospel. The Oxford Group, in his opinion, had done this and had given him a new secular ministry by its fresh approach to the tasks of Christian living. Yet this new "secular ministry" had not led him to sully the Church of Norway's continued importance in his spiritual development:

> I know full well that Christianity has developed particular forms in differ-
> ent lands…I love our Church of Norway, our hymns, our religious folk tunes.
> I never listen to Lindemann's Chorales without rejoicing over how genuinely
> Norwegian they are (p. 121).

Yet Buchman's "international army of Christians" had impressed him because it
proclaimed Christian universality amidst the competing and divisive groups he
saw within the Lutheran community. By this time Fangen had gained a reputation as a stimulating "academic lay preacher" and he became a popular speaker at
Christian youth meetings.[10]

Sigmund Mowinckel wrote about his new spiritual attitude that had resulted
from the contact he made with Buchman and his followers:

> I saw more clearly than ever before…that my so-called intellectual difficul-
> ties concerning faith in God were actually a cover for something else, namely,
> an unwillingness to see my sin and to surrender both it and myself to God.[11]

Eivind Berggrav contributed to the discussion in an article in <u>Church and Cul-
ture</u>. He describes the Group as a "source of power" instead of a model for Christian living. With a critical eye he examined the impact and methods employed by
the Group as they related to the Church of Norway. Praising "Oxford's openness
and cheerfulness," Berggrav denounces the reluctance of Christians in Norway to
speak openly about their beliefs. Yet he argues that for Christians to copy the
Group methods in a mechanical way would be neither biblical nor evangelical for
not all Christians can become "life-changers." The question is not if believers are
going to be "Groupers," he insisted, it is rather whether they are going to be
Christians. For this reason, the message of the Group was to be taken more seriously than its methods. Berggrav was thankful for the good impulse to Church
life in Norway that had resulted from many Norwegian houseparties: "Oxford is
not a new model but an old source of power."[12]

The success of the Group in Norway was greatly aided by men who, like Fangen, had been loyal to the Church of Norway and who also possessed theological
insight: the bishop Eivind Berggrav, the missionary Sten Bugge, and professors
Eiliv Skard and Sigmund Mowinckel. Christians in Norway had been challenged
by the enthusiasm of the Groupers and by their insistence upon definite activities
to mark the life of a Christian. Einar Molland writes that the Group's campaign
in Norway established a more cordial relationship with the Church than had
been the case in other European countries; many of the "changed" became regu-
lar churchgoers and communicants.[13]

The Group houseparty appeared to Fangen to be a workable method for inspiring Christian laymen to engage in a secular ministry of the Church. Rather than having encouraged him to separate from the Church of Norway, he insisted that the Group had renewed his love for it:

> I love our Church...but it has become foreign for many modern people who simply cannot understand its language...The Church also needs moments of confession of sin. When they come, the Church is renewed. I believe it is happening now.[14]

Before his "change" at Høsbjør, however, he had been committed to the Church in a more passive and intellectual manner. From now on he would actively invite others to join a "Christian world revolution."

10
TO THE SKEPTICS

By 1934 Ronald Fangen's writings won wide recognition in Norway. Although critics had shown that only a few of his works had genuine literary merit, several of his books had become best sellers and he had served as chairman of The Norwegian Author's Association (Den norske forfatterforening).[15] In his early publications Fangen stresses social and political aspects of Scandinavian culture. Later on, particularly in the novels he wrote from 1929 to 1934, he concentrates more upon the spiritual struggles of the characters he portrays. This change of emphasis is accompanied by an analysis of leading Biblical motifs: sin, redemption, and freedom. As a Christian humanist the author delves into the relationship between historic Christianity and man's culture.

After his involvement with the Oxford Group Movement, Fangen intensified his interest in a Christian world-view; he became both intellectually and emotionally involved with the Christian religion, and he attempted to convert "outsiders" to the style of Christian faith he had recently experienced.

The drama, As it Went and as it Might Have Gone (Som det gikk og som det kunde ha gått), is his first attempt to communicate the Christian gospel through an artistic means. "As it Went" describes the tragic break-up of the characters as they ignore Christian morality. "As it Might Have Gone" speculates upon the degrees of rehabilitation the Christian faith might have brought them. The author's recent "Oxford" experience is evident in the play: sins are confessed, "sharing" is described and there are numerous references to passages from the Bible.[16]

The drama suffers greatly because of an artistic weakness; its characters appear as puppets in the hands of the playwright. Rather than permitting the audience to share their existence vicariously, Fangen maneuvers them about in the direction of publicizing the effectiveness of Oxford Group techniques in solving personal problems. It was sharply criticized in the Oslo press after its performance in the National Theatre. Einar Skavlan wrote that the play used

> dramatized revival language which made a Prayer Chapel (bedehus) out of the Theatre. Has Fangen by a miracle become someone completely different: not a writer, only a lay preacher?[17]

In commenting upon the effort Fangen made to employ his literary talent in promoting the Group's cause, Frank Buchman wrote:

> The thing that he often spoke of was having reached a point of deadness in his writing, when every problem had been analyzed and dramatized. Then suddenly with his own change there opened up to him a new field of writing where, instead of glamorizing the problem, he found the way to dramatize the answer.[18]

The "new field of writing" introduced by <u>As it Went and as it Might Have Gone</u> did not win Fangen the respect of two of his literary colleagues, Helge Krog and Arnulf Øverland, both of whom were highly skeptical of the significance of the Oxford Group's impact in Norway. Øverland had this to say in a letter to the writer:

> He [Fangen] had great energy for work, was very well read and had a lively intellect. As young people we were friends, but differences in political views began to separate us, and his religious conversion to Frank Buchman made continued association unsatisfactory for both parties. Afterwards his writing did not interest me very much either.[19]

The failure of the play did not deter Fangen from continuing an attempt to convince his readers of the validity of a Høsbjør-type religious experience. His next work, a novel, is also sympathetic to the Oxford Group. <u>The Disillusioned</u> (<u>På bar bunn</u>) appeared the following year.[20] Among its characters are a physician, an editor, a youthful intellectual, and a pastor. All are disillusioned with life. With the exception of the pastor, they do not believe in God. But they do not believe in anything else either—in humanity, their careers, or in their own capacities. The young intellectual, Sven Bauk, is proud of his freedom from moral restrictions. He does not love his wife, Ruth, and when he admits being unfaithful to her, comments, "I intended no harm to her. I act freely and must live my own life…I build upon nothing…. This is a law of nature" (pp. 67,83). Yet his renunciation of moral principle does not bring happiness. Sven seeks further meaning in life. (p. 135). At the extremity of his disillusionment with his existence, an awareness of childhood learning about God and the Bible begins to dawn upon him. After a profound self-examination, he determines to live as a Christian (pp. 176–79).

There are apparent references to Oxford Group techniques in <u>The Disillusioned</u>. The pastor, Anders Venger, is given new inspiration as a result of an "honest" self-examination of his life (pp. 142–55, 295–96). Sven Bauk decides to live as a Christian, and meditates:

> Then he suddenly understood in a new way who Christ was: that he was God who met men…in deepest corruption, at the end of the rope (på bar bunn), Christ in the form of men, as servant of all (p. 294).

Just at the moment he decides to follow a new way of faith, Anders Venger comes, having been "guided" to speak with Sven about his anxiety (p. 296).

The Disillusioned helped restore Fangen's prestige as a writer. Sigurd Hoel declared that its early chapters were the best written of all the author's works. But, to his view, the book was "religious propaganda":

> As we all know, Fangen has had a great, and, for him, a decisive religious experience. As we also know, he feels a compulsion and a mission to give others a share in this experience.[21]

Inge Debes and Kristian Elster criticized the author for maneuvering his characters toward the solution to life's meaninglessness offered by Christianity. They insisted that this solution was too simple. "It is difficult to be a preacher and an artist at the same time," wrote Eugenia Kielland, "…in this book Fangen is a preacher."[22] One must agree with these critics concerning the artistry of the novel; its story, however, grips the mind of the reader with the author's conviction that it is essential for man to have some basis in life, something to build his existence upon. Fangen had effectively portrayed his interpretation of the anxiety resulting from a self-centered existence.

In 1937 Fangen published Right Now (Allerede nu) as a sequel to Some Young People, Erik, and The Disillusioned.[23] Right Now continues a portrayal of the leading characters in these novels, and the author intended to complete his cycle with still another novel (p. 384). The artistic ability that Fangen displayed in such novels as Duel and The Man Who Loved Righteousness is not evident in this novel, as Carl Fredrik Engelstad has pointed out.[24] It does, however, disclose an insight into the author's understanding of Christianity shortly following his association with the Oxford Group Movement.

In Right Now Erik experiences a Christian "break-through to faith" brought about by the illness of Astrid, his wife, and by the patient Christian counsel of the pastor, Toralf Holm. Erik learned that he needed God's support in the face of Astrid's illness, and that "he could not help himself…" (p. 379). Following Erik's decision to believe in God, Holm reflects:

> Christ's love is the lifting of men up out of themselves; it discloses a way out
> from the world of death to paradise and holiness…Right now he could feel
> the power from him who called himself the resurrection and the life in his
> own being, and in the lives of others. Right now. Right here! And this was
> only a beginning…(pp. 382–83).

Sven Bauk makes a similar commitment at the close of The Disillusioned. In Right Now his effort to live a Christian way of life is portrayed. Sven's intellectual associates view Christianity as obscurantic and take his new stand to be scandalous. But he receives encouragement to continue because he believes God's Spirit is at work in his life (pp. 61–67). When Sven seeks to put his faith into practice by seeking to make an Oxford Group "restitution" in asking another person's forgiveness, George, his brother, coldly rebuffs him. But Sven is able to accept the experience as a lesson in Christian obedience (pp. 162–70).

Anders Venger, a pastor, goes to his bishop to make restitution. This unusual gesture comes as a result of his new and dynamic understanding of Christianity. The bishop, however, takes Venger's new attitude as a threat to established Church procedures and perceives him to be under the influence of "the unevangelical and dangerous Anglo-Saxon Group Movement" (pp. 148–59). Venger replies that he has read several books about the Oxford Group Movement, and expresses his endorsement of it, because, in his view, the Movement demonstrated the principles of the Kingdom of God. Furthermore, he maintains that the Groupers had stimulated a national interest in Christian unity. Venger can no longer live "secure behind the walls of the Church" because of his conviction that the Church must confront men personally with the Kingdom of God. Far from being a threat to the theology and practice of the Church, Venger insists that the Movement can renew his beloved Church. The bishop strongly disagrees, and Venger, like Sven Bauk, experienced the pain of Christian obedience (pp. 160–61).

Bible citations in Right Now support the descriptions of sharing and restitution, as well as the more characteristic Oxford Group principles of "surrender" and "life changing." To Venger, the essence of one's "surrender" involved the consciousness of the dynamics of the Kingdom of God:

> To be a Christian intellectual was not the same as being a Christian disciple.
> The Gospel concerns something quite different. It concerns Christ's Kingdom; it concerns the grace which allows a sinful and lost person to receive life
> and the power to follow after Christ, and to live in fellowship with him. But

the qualification was this: obedience, surrender—the willingness to lose one's life in order to win it. (pp. 139–40).

Philip Houm declared that the portrayals of the clergymen in Right Now offered a valuable insight into the religious and theological conflicts of the time. Together with other critics, however, he opposed the novel's Christian flavor. One must agree with Einar Skavlan that its dialogues might well have been written for a parish publication, and that the author once more sacrificed his artistic integrity to his zeal to promote the Group cause.[26]

In 1939 The Citizen's Holiday (Borgerfesten) appeared. It is the first novel of an uncompleted cycle entitled The Mill That Grinds Slowly (Kvernen som maler langsomt).[27] The background of The Citizen's Holiday is the city of Bergen, where Fangen had lived as a youth. In this novel the characters occasionally deliver what appear to be short sermons in which the author outlines again the religious convictions he expressed in The Disillusioned and Right Now.

The novels discussed above reveal a change in the author's Christian conviction following his association with the Oxford Group Movement. In earlier novels, Fangen's characters are isolated individuals who wrestle with the task of justifying their existence. They learn that before God justification is not a matter of their own achievement; instead, it is God's gift. Having been declared righteous by God, they perceive a way to new life and hope. Here the portrayals of George Røiter in Duel and of Gottfried Stein in The Man Who Loved Righteousness end. In the novels Fangen wrote during the years from 1934 to 1940, however, the leading characters are portrayed in the process of growing in their knowledge of God and of themselves. Such is the case with Sven Bauk in The Disillusioned and Anders Venger in Right Now. One result of this growth is that they no longer remain isolated from other Christians because, together with them, they seek to share a new view of life with "the disillusioned."

11

TO THE CHURCH

Fangen also wrote many essays, sermons, and devotional meditations during the years from 1934 to 1940. In them he made an appeal, for the most part, to other Christians in Norway.

The Lutheran Church of Norway differs from Lutheran church bodies in America because of its official ties with the Kingdom of Norway. The "Church" in Norway normally refers to the official State Church organization, controlled by Parliament through a Minister of Ecclesiastical Affairs and the King, in which most Norwegians are baptized, confirmed, wed, and buried.[28]

When King Olaf Haraldsson enacted legislation in 1024 in which Christianity was established as a national religion, the Church of Norway was born.[29] Following the Reformation, the Lutheran worship and a new church organization were formally established during the reign of Christian III in 1537. Today, eighty-six per cent of Norway's population belong nominally to the State Church. Within the last decades the Church of Norway has adapted itself to modern needs by revising its liturgy and hymnody, and by experimenting in new forms of Church art and architecture.[30]

Within the Church of Norway, however, are those who look beyond their official ties with religion to smaller associations in which one's personal commitment to Christianity may be expressed. Hence, vigorous independent groups carry out extensive missionary work within Norway and upon foreign fields. Among Christians in Norway, therefore, there is a duality of loyalty towards the official Church, its worship and its life, and towards the more intimate communities of those actively committed to the Christian cause. Thus, personal commitment is a decisive factor in the Norwegian understanding of Christianity.

Fangen delves into the subject of personal commitment in Some Young People. In the lengthy theological dialogue between Toralf Holm and Erik Hamre, Holm voices his displeasure of the "vanekristen" (conventional Christian), the one whose faith is merely a matter of form and habit. He is convinced that he has never been a Christian, and that the reality of faith would have to come with "a break, a conversion" (pp. 59–82). Erik, content to remain a "conventional Christian," cannot understand Toralf's feelings (p. 91). In Erik, the sequel to Some Young People, however, Toralf Holm's affirmation of the Christian gospel in word and deed conquers the indifference of Erik Hamre. In these portrayals Fangen may be expressing his own search for a more vital Christian commitment.

In the sense that he became involved in a religious re-orientation of his attitude toward life, Fangen had been "converted" at Høsbjør. But despite the fact that he experienced this reorientation within a small circle of Oxford Group followers, Fangen did not renounce his association with the Church of Norway. On the contrary, he entered publicly into its activity. His awakened interest in the Church stimulated his study of the Bible and of Christian theology.

Paul and Our Own Time (Paulus og vår egen tid), written to popularize Bible study among Group converts, reveals the author's debt to the Apostle. In this book Fangen describes the "human" side of St. Paul; according to Fangen's view, St. Paul was not an "abstract" theologian because the great themes of his theology—sin, salvation, the Spirit, love—were rooted in his experience.

In the account of St. Paul's conversion, Fangen found parallels to the Oxford Group practices of guidance, life-changing, and sharing:

> All Christians live in fellowship, and no one can be a Christian without participation in a community, the destiny of which concerns all men, and most of all those who labor to create and to uphold it.[31]

By his missionary zeal, the Apostle had shared Christ's sufferings for the world. And the modern Church, Fangen contends, must also see this task as decisive to its existence. Divisions in the Church thwart this effort, however, and cause the Church to become self-centered (pp. 27–37).

Fangen admits that theological issues, such as the relationship between God's law and God's grace, had previously been "dry symbols," but now he, like the Apostle, had experienced a religious awakening after having surrendered to God's will for daily living; "For Paul, the Christian life is controlled by God, and the Christian man is one who submits to the guidance of God" (pp. 49,66).

Yet submission to the guidance of God is not always easy; St. Paul's description of the Christian life does not concern

> religious patent medicine which…one-two-three saves us…and hocus pocus makes us now men…Christianity is in its deepest sense as paradoxical and as irrational as life itself (pp. 80,89).

This does not mean, however, that "reason should be cast aside and matters calling for understanding be neglected in the Christian life (p. 81). "St. Paul," he concluded, "had shown men genuine Christian love. But are modern Christians willing to follow his example?" (pp. 140–41).

Fangen had begun to underscore his new attitude toward the Christian faith. Although orthodox, his attitude was antagonistic to any type of orthodoxy which instead of making faith a relationship of trust in God, tended instead to make it an intellectual assent to statements about that relationship:

> Taken as a whole, Christianity is not faith in this or that teaching, but it is faith in Christ, he who is much greater than dogmas and who, among other things, has promised that whosoever believes in him shall have everlasting life.[32]

Fangen's loyalty to the State Church of Norway following his association with the Oxford Group Movement is evident in articles he wrote for Signs of the Times in 1936.[33] But he lamented the signs of disunity in the Church. His support of a positive, ecumenical point of view verifies the comment of Johannes Lavik:

> He was fully and completely at home in the Church of Norway, but his ecumenical perspective was soon broadened. He was one of our few ecumenics.[34]

Ecumenism in Norway, Fangen maintained, had been hindered by the development of Christian factions which stressed personal religious experience above the worship life of the congregation.[35]

In Lutheran tradition, a one-sided emphasis upon spiritual experience in the life of the Christian is "checked" by means of the sacraments. Insofar as ceremonies are connected with the administration of the sacraments, Luther acknowledged their rightful place in worship.[36] The Augsburg Confession states that the public worship of the congregation has a pedagogical function and is to be retained.[37] Fangen did not permit his association with the Oxford Group to alter his loyalty to the Lutheran understanding of the importance of worship and the administration of the sacraments. It is in this tradition, he insists, that one may experience the "majesty" of Christian unity.[38]

The Christian factions which stressed personal religious experience also emphasized the importance of preaching. As far as this emphasis was concerned, Fangen wrote:

> I will not attack the sermon in any sense. But a one-sided preaching Church is not, according to my understanding, a Church...Our worship services are

lacking in quiet times, in times set aside for devotion and adoration. I admire the Catholic Church because it is a sacramental Church.[39]

He regretted that one of these factions, the Inner Mission Society, held a negative attitude toward the Oxford Group Movement. "One would like to believe," he wrote, "that the religion of reconciliation should create reconciliation among those who committed themselves to it."[40]

In 1935 Fangen thought that the Oxford Group Movement heralded a Christian renascence on a world-wide scale. To this end he advocated dialogue between Protestants and Catholics. "The time has come," he wrote, "for Christians of all denominations to speak out to one another in order to advance toward the goal Christ has set: Christian unity."[41] Together with his friends, Arne Fjelberg and Fredrik Ramm, Fangen attended an ecumenical conference in Sweden in 1936. A lecture he delivered at the conference, <u>Christian Unity</u> (<u>Kristen enhet</u>), was published the following year.[42]

In this lecture Fangen discloses that one of the features of the Høsbjør houseparty which attracted him most was the ecumenical make-up of the international team which sponsored it. The team had shown him that Christians from many nations and denominations could stand united in faith, and it had inspired him to want to share such an attitude. He wrote:

> I am not paid by the Group, but I thank it for helping me take the Christian commitment I had so longed to take earlier. God himself must defend the Group from all forms of pride and self-satisfaction (p. 45).

The cause of Christian unity must first concern individuals, Fangen maintains, and a frank acknowledgement of sin is the starting point for ecumenism. By its technique of confession, the Group had presented a useful way to begin. He quoted a Group slogan in this regard: "Sin is everything that separates men from God and from each other." (p. 36). Moving from individual confession, and individual faith in Christ, ecumenism might then concern denonominations and Christian factions. Fangen asked Lutheran pastors to support an Oxford Group orientated attitude towards Christian unity. By evaluating the Group's techniques, and by increasing their concern for individual "soul care," pastors, he asserted, could help "remove the wall which too often isolated clergy and laity."[43]

The factions which had developed within the Church were not the only threat to the proclamation of its Gospel; from "without," Nazism and Bolshevism also posed a threat to the Church.[44] Thus Fangen rejoiced in the efforts toward Christian unity which were at that time evident to him:

> That we belong to different churches does not hinder our feeling of unity in the divinity of Christ...The work to create this unity, the ecumenical movement, is being carried forward in these times with great intensity and faith. It is one of the most encouraging things that is happening.[45]

During the years following the Høsbjør experience, Fangen had broken out from his intellectually isolated association with the Church into the fellowship of those who were actively involved in its life.

12

THE SEARCH FOR RELEVANCE

Today, as perhaps never before, the Christian Church faces profound challenges to a number of its foundations of faith and life. What, for instance, does the command to "be fruitful and multiply" (Genesis 1:28) mean in a world threatened by overpopulation? What is the nature of premarital chastity when the birth-control pill has made sexual intercourse without fear of pregnancy a universal possibility? How shall the injunction "Let every person be subject to the governing authorities" (Romans 13:1) be understood in the light of current agitation for the right of "selective conscientious objectors"? What do Jesus' words about the "lilies of the field and the birds of the air" (Matthew 6: 25f.) mean to people in the midst of famine, or to a government laying out long-range economic plans? What becomes of the Biblical "peace among men" (Luke 2:14) in the face of Viet Nam, Chad, and the Middle East? And with what means shall the Church seek to implement the Biblical "There is neither Jew nor Greek, slave nor free..." (Galatians 3:28) in the global combat against racism?

Christianity and Our Times (Kristendommen og vår tid) contains Fangen's analysis of pre Second World War political and social problems from his interpretation of the Christian point of view.[46] Subsequent history has shown that the issues with which he wrestled in this book were of enormous importance, and continue so today. In these essays, he stresses that the Christian faith claims the "total man," and that it concerns all aspects of his existence. It was, therefore, obligatory for the Christian to suggest means for resolving political and social issues. Fangen asserts that insights concerning Christ, and the believer's fellowship with his Lord, hold the key to solving such issues. Each person involved in this tension must choose between allegiance to Christ, and allegiance to "false gods" (p. 47).

The most dangerous "false god" is nationalism. Fangen argues that nationalism distorts the religious insight of God's universal rule over mankind. In 1938, he viewed with alarm the relationship between nationalism and the preparations for war. After the Munich agreement he wrote:

> I thank God because he has answered the prayers of millions of people that war's unthinkable terrors be averted. I feel as if God has given the world a respite, one more delay, to search for peace. Otherwise the war must come (p. 53).

German National Socialism is singled out by the author as an example of a false god. In this system, Christ was made to serve the aims of the German nation. Christ, however, is the mediator between God and all mankind. Glorying in its nationalistic pride and selfishness, Germany had given birth to two ominous facts: concentration camps, and race war against the Jews. The resulting "holocaust" of the Second World War in which six million Jews perished became the terrible verification of the author's analysis.

Another false god of the nineteen-thirties was Communism, which also constituted a threat to Christianity:

> Ultimately it must be said that Communism breaks with Christianity and declares war against it, because, like National Socialism, it is a religion and confronts men with a total appeal and claim (p. 99).

The religion of Communism, unlike Christianity, placed the value of the collective above the value of the individual. But "collective social justice," Fangen wrote, "is unthinkable apart from respect and love for the individual" (p. 119). He supported an individual's equal worth before God. It alone can fulfill man's desire for peace and security (p. 111).

Democracy and humanism also came under Fangen's censure (pp. 120–36). Democracy did not hinder men from acknowledging God; unlike totalitarianism, it made no religious claim upon one's total loyalty. But democracy had fostered class distinctions, and it possessed no dynamic to cope with moral crises. Humanism, which Fangen defined as "a respect for all men and everything human," was a "religion of humanity" (p. 128). It heralded an unrealistic faith in the goodness of man and in the idea of progress, he maintained, because both democracy and humanism had failed to take seriously-enough the religious insight concerning sin:

> In the last analysis <u>sin</u>, not <u>sins</u> is the essence of the Christian view of man—sin in all men and in all forms, individual and collective, the <u>evil</u>. Not even the noblest of men are free from sin (p. 131).

To the author's view, Christianity provided man with the best possibility for dealing realistically with problems concerning human nature and society.

In the essay, "The Way of Christianity" ("Kristendommens vei"), he outlines his view of Christian ethics as a way of "inner freedom," being bound, like St. Paul, to higher values and goals. Living under the Lordship of Christ one was "born anew," illuminated by Christian truth, and upheld by faith. Having this attitude, the Christian may love his neighbor and come to grips with problems in human society (pp. 148–50).

The content of <u>Christianity and Our Time</u>, Fangen wrote, was based upon his own experience of attempting to live the Christian way of life; he acknowledges no indebtedness to the Oxford Group Movement for his Christian convictions.[47]

Three emphases are apparent in his interpretation of the relevance of Christianity to his time. First is his emphasis upon the Lutheran understanding of the term "Gospel."[48] The creative source of the Church arises not so much from a common experience as from a common Gospel. This Gospel, the gift of God in Christ, has an objective reality apart from human acceptance or rejection of it. His Oxford Group experience stimulated Fangen's appreciation of this Gospel, but he maintained that the Church, the Bible, and Christian experience point beyond themselves to its authority.

Second is his emphasis upon the Lutheran understanding of the term "sin."[49] The depths of sin in the human situation are illustrated by the Cross of Christ. It stands as a judgment upon one's sin but also as a source of forgiveness and new life. Joy for this salvation is the motive for ethical behavior.[50] Yet an ethic which changed only the individual is inadequate because the individual is inextricably bound to society. If the social system in which one is involved promoted injustice and intolerance, then the Christian must resist it as an avenue of one of sin's destructive inroads upon man's spiritual potential. When one becomes wholly engaged in living as a Christian, he discovers a universal brotherhood; he is enlightened by God's revelation in Christ, and, with fellow believers, he shares a hope of God's ultimate victory over sin.

Thirdly, Fangen emphasized that there could be no rigid Christian attitude toward specific ethical problems. The Gospel gives one the ability to reorientate one's life, but the Christian life is a constant process of growth toward Christian maturity. New situations and new problems must call forth from the Christian a fresh response and self-examination. Rarely did Fangen refer to the experiences of Christians in past centuries in the struggle between faith and culture; the Gospel, he insists, must speak with relevance to each generation. <u>Christianity and Our Time</u> is the author's witness to that relevance for his generation.

The Oxford Group influence upon this book is not as apparent as Egil Elseth suggests.[51] By 1938 the "MRA" phase of the Movement had been introduced, and in 1940 T.S. Eliot commented that this change resulted in the Movement's marked separation from the historic Christian faith toward its development of a type of religious enthusiasm adapted to fit secular aims.[52] Although the Oxford

Group had stimulated Fangen's study of the Bible as well as his active association with the Church, <u>Kristendommen og vår tid</u> shows that by 1938 he was already intellectually independent of it.

The war between Russia and Finland is the setting for <u>War and Christian Faith</u> (<u>Krig og kristen tro</u>). In this book Fangen continues his discussion of the relationship between culture and the Christian religion. In order to eliminate war, a symptom of man's distorted relationship with the material world, Fangen asserts that the fountainhead of all war be unmasked. This fountainhead, he believed, was the evil power of man's sin (pp. 14–17). Sin, in its cosmic dimension, holds sway over all mankind. But God is at work to redeem man from its power by uniting all peoples and races at the end of time (p. 63). This union has already begun in the Church, the "communion of saints," which is a spiritual community surpassing ties of family and nationality (p. 66). Fangen is convinced that the urgent task confronting the Church is to strengthen its unity in order that a "decisive step on the way to reconciliation among nations" might be taken (p. 71). The state is a provisional part of God's final purpose, and he objects to any government which interferes with the divine order of the Kingdom of God by making totalitarian claims. When the state did not assert such claims, the Christian might "coexist" with it and even fight to defend it. This is because in Christ the "end of time" is already present. But the consummation of the "end of time" is yet to come, and it is for this reason that the framework of the present world endures.[54]

Carl Fredrik Engelstad is correct in declaring that <u>War and Christian Faith</u> shows that the author had greatly qualified the Christian optimism which he revealed in earlier "Oxford" writings such as <u>The New Life</u> and <u>A Christian World Revolution</u>.[55]

Concerning this earlier optimistic point of view Fangen had this to say:

> In my first years as a committed Christian I believed most in the way of progress. It is such an overpowering experience to comprehend Christianity's saving truth that one cannot help believing in its quick victory through man's free decision and commitment...When I no longer possess such Christian optimism it is not because the truth of Christianity is less clear to me...it comes because now, in a new and deeper way, I understand the power of evil in the world.[56]

The years 1934 to 1940 were of lasting importance in Fangen's spiritual development. The Høsbjør experience had given him a new and lasting religious orientation. Impending events, however would soon deepen his religious experience and quicken his search for values the Group Movement no longer provided.

4

LENGTHENING SHADOWS
1940–1946

o o o o o o o o o o o o o o o o o o o o o o o o o o o o o o o o o
"Yea, in the day of trouble, he will hide me in his tabernacle."

—Psalm 27:5

13
PRISON

At the outbreak of the Second World War in 1939, Fangen voiced his despair with these words:

> The great war which we have seen coming and dreaded for so long a time has arrived. All strivings of man to save the world from catastrophe have shown themselves to be in vain. We have less reason than ever to cultivate an optimistic view concerning this world and to underestimate the power of evil.[1]

The hostilities which engulfed Norway in April, 1940, intensified his religious conviction that God's purpose for man would ultimately prevail:

> Today there are many of our great words which fade in our mouths; spiritual life, culture, human worth. We have believed in the magic power of these words and that they could placate evil powers. It was an illusion. We have reason to be pessimistic about our ways and those things which belong to this world. Yet we need not be pessimistic about God's Spirit. Cultural epochs disappear, secularized life, bound to shifting social systems, bears the seeds of its destruction. Yet God's Spirit remains Lord of all.[2]

When the Germans completed their occupation of Norway, Fangen limited his comments about the dramatic turn of events to a broad religious interpretation of them. To his view, the war was an eschatological event which testified to the solidarity of mankind in sin and it revealed that man's efforts to find meaning in life apart from God were all in vain.[3]

From a more positive stance, he emphasized faith's blessings in a devotion written for the Ringsaker parish paper. In faith the Christian perceived the changing nature of the world and trusted the promise of Christ, "the same yesterday, today, and forever" (Hebrews 13:8). "The times of catastrophe and destruction," he wrote, "reveal our faith to be the only security we possess."[4] In September, 1940, he published a patriotic poem, "To Once More Rebuild the Nation" ("Å bygge landet op igjen"), which brought no unfavorable reaction from the occupation forces because it contained no apparent antagonism toward them.[5] An article which appeared the following month, however, stirred an immediate response from the German authorities and led its author into a period of crisis and conflict.

"Concerning Faithfullness" ("Om troskap") has a religious content similar to Fangen's other articles written during the early months of the occupation, but it also contains political overtones.[6] The article cites the German philosopher Fichte's reaction against the Napoleonic occupation of Germany and hints that the occupation of Norway paralleled the action Fichte denounced.

Fangen's arrest followed swiftly. Early in November he was visiting in Oslo, and had made an appointment to meet a friend, Odd Eidem, in a downtown restaurant. When Fangen did not appear, Eidem began to inquire about him. He telephoned Fangen's Oxford Group friend, Erling Wikborg, who joined Eidem and Solveig Fangen at the restaurant. As Mrs. Fangen's anxiety grew, Eidem went to the German headquarters at the Victoria Terrace police station. In response to his inquiry about his friend an angry officer shouted, "Leave here or we'll take you in too! Ronald Fangen is where he ought to be." This meant the prison at Møllergaten 19. Eidem hurried back to inform his friends.[7]

Immediately Wikborg arranged for Mrs. Fangen's departure on the night train for Dusgård. He instructed her to destroy any of her husband's letters or documents which would implicate his friends in regard to the content of the article, "Om troskap." That same night, from one until four in the morning, she and her son-in-law followed Wikborg's instructions and buried a number of letters with incriminating evidence. By eight o'clock the next morning (November 9) five German soldiers came to search Dusgård. They investigated Fangen's library of nearly ten thousand volumes and, Solveig Fangen recalled, were especially interested in its Oxford Group literature. She also related how surprised she was that they overlooked a letter from Eivind Berggrav, in plain view on the desk, which would have further implicated her husband with the resistance movement.[8] Although his essay was the immediate reason for his arrest, Fangen had already been under surveillance by the Germans because of his friendship with Berggrav and because of a patriotic sermon he had delivered earlier that fall in Bergen.[9]

Having been locked in a solitary cell, the prisoner tried to adjust to his grim new existence. Three days after his arrival, his first letter reached Dusgård:

> I am now in prison and do not know for how long. Remain here in town. You can stay at the Wikborg's...I hope the baggage has not gone back to Ring. Be calm. I am calm. God bless you.[10]

The following week Fangen had received a letter from his wife as well as medicine and clothing. He responded by assuring his family he was being well treated, and by expressing his gratitude for the kindness his friends had shown to them. He added:

> And God is with me. I feel myself <u>undergirded</u> by prayers, and now I have such a wonderful opportunity to pray myself. Do you know what the first word of Scripture that I meditated upon here in the cell was? It was Job 8:21 ("He will yet fill your mouth with laughter and your lips with shouting").[11]

Toward the end of November a close relative of Fangen's died in Bergen. When Bishop Berggrav went to Møllergaten 19 to bring him the news, he noticed a red tag, which designated maximum security, fastened to the door of the cell. Outside the cell door Berggrav read from the New Testament and heard the prisoner begin to pray out loud. Although they had been ordered to speak German, nothing happened when, "with hands folded and with uplifted face, the prisoner prayed in the language of his heart."[12]

Soon afterward, in a letter to his wife Fangen mentioned that confinement had affected his nerves and that it had brought him "a bit of my old stomach pain"; but the doctor had prescribed effective medicine, and his physical condition was satisfactory. He was hopeful that his case might be considered before Christmas time. And although he longed to see his family, he was confident:

"Rest assured that I am all right—everything <u>surely</u> will be settled very soon."[13]

Several days later Solveig Fangen visited her husband. At that time he still did not know what the charges against him were, and he saw little hope of being released before the new year. He had written to the German authorities to explain the situation from his point of view, but he received only a guarantee of medical attention from them. Having only a Bible and a hymnbook in his cell, Fangen asked his wife to try to obtain more reading material for him. As Christmas drew near, the prisoner's health condition deteriorated and he longed to be released to Ullevål Hospital. In a Christmas letter to his family at Dusgård, he wrote, "Enjoy yourselves and remember the one in Møllergaten 19 or in Ullevål who loves you and prays for you all."[14]

Life in prison afforded time for prayer and meditation. In an untitled and unfinished poem he reflected:

Lord, you know. You surely know all.
Why should I speak to you this
way—about myself—my life, my being?

Not to tell you something you do not know,
But because you know all about it,
—better than I, and understand it better than I.
Therefore it is with <u>you</u> I must speak,

Of what use is it to speak with all
those who do not know themselves and
are filled only with themselves.[15]

When Fangen learned that his case would not be considered until after New Year's, he despaired in a letter to his wife, "All this wasted time…I understand less and less about this whole matter." He thanked his family for their Christmas letter and praised the sermon Bishop Berggrav had delivered at the prison Christmas observance. He closed:

So we shall not be able to spend New Year's Eve together. I cannot manage to write any New Year's letter-you know it all without my saying it…sometime I will come to know the meaning—even of this.[16]

During December Berggrav visited Fangen several times in his cell; on one of these occasions he smuggled out another poem the prisoner had written entitled, "Passion" ("Pasjon"). It is a meditation upon the suffering of Jesus. In the last stanza, the author expressed his Christian hope:

You, Lord, are the certainty. You are the clear message from him who no one here can see: the light encircled, hidden God.

We see you, Lord. And I know that at the end of my way, when this heart's anxiety dies—then I shall meet you.[17]

Fangen was the first Norwegian author imprisoned during the occupation; his arrest soon became known throughout Norway and it helped solidify Norwegian resistance to the German forces. His Oxford Group friend, Fredrik Ramm, who would also be imprisoned, informed Fangen of his new fame. After the war Fangen commented about this and wrote, "I was not supposed to believe that I was not doing my work in that place—it was a first class piece of work!"[18]

In January Fangen was moved to Ullevål Hospital in Oslo. The solitary cell and the anxiety caused by the uncertainty of judgment had been a severe strain. Another of his Oxford Group friends, Einar Lundby, was able to visit him there because he was a physician. Fangen related that the cries and pleas of other prisoners in Møllergaten 19 had made his stay there especially "difficult on his nerves," but the reason for his being sent to the hospital was the recurrence of his gall bladder trouble.[19]

On February 11, 1941, Victor Mogens, a friend from the time of the First World War, wrote to Reichskommissar Terboven and asked for Fangen's release. Mogens stated that he had not had any dealings with Fangen after the author had associated himself with the Oxford Group Movement, and he listed several reasons why he thought Fangen should be released. First, he insisted that Fangen was a "psychological" writer; hence his knowledge of political affairs was limited. Second, Mogens reported that the prisoner's German physician had already suggested his release. Third, according to Mogens, Fangen had become a "propaganda martyr" both within and without the borders of Norway. Furthermore, Mogens offered a financial guarantee that his friend would not attempt to leave Norway upon his release, and that he would in the future not concern himself with political matters in his speaking and writing. He closed the letter by writing that he understood Knut Hamsun had sent Terboven a similar appeal.[20]

But the letter had no effect and Fangen remained under guard at Ullevål. At the end of February he was more reconciled to his circumstance:

> We must also think about the fact that there is so much unbounded suffering in this world now; it would not have been right if we, too, had not gotten our share of it—'Suffering works patience, and patience a proven mind.' I preach for myself, you understand![21]

Months passed; in June his family received a letter in which he praised the medical attention he was getting. Despite this, however, he was "too tired" and not well enough to do any work. The next day the family was surprised to receive another letter in which he expressed confidence that his case would be settled shortly, and that he would soon be on his way home.[22] Fangen's release came on June 24. Øivind Berggrav, son of the Bishop, met him at the hospital and escorted him to Dusgård, where he lived for the remainder of the occupation.[23]

During these months of anguish Fangen made no mention in his letters of any comfort he derived from practicing Oxford Group techniques such as "guidance" and "sharing." He apparently made no attempts to "change lives" in prison, and his letters contain no Oxford Group slogans of optimism and personal confidence. Rather, he learned from this trying experience that suffering may also be a part of a Christian's calling; in his reflections upon the sufferings of his Lord he had drawn strength from the more meaningful Christian insights of faith and hope.

14
HOME AT DUSGÅRD

In order to recuperate from the eight-month ordeal in prison Fangen needed complete rest. The rustic setting of his home at Dusgård, overlooking Lake Mjøsa, afforded an ideal place for him to renew his strength. Built around 1850, the beautiful and spacious frame home was the former parsonage of the Ringsaker parish. Several desks were located next to windows overlooking the majestic lake and hills beyond. There, surrounded by hundreds of his books, Fangen would write. During the course of the day he would move his work to that desk most illuminated by the sun.[24]

Although he was unable to work for the remainder of 1941, Fangen welcomed visitors and corresponded with friends as the condition of his health gradually improved. Among his frequent visitors at Dusgård during the years of the occupation from 1941 to 1945 were Stephan Tschudi and Harald Hille. From Fangen's correspondence with these and other friends, and from their recollections of conversations with him, one learns about Fangen's vision of the tasks and the opportunities which he believed would confront the Church in post-war Norway.

One task would involve the establishment of better Church unity. Another would concern the formulation of a more positive witness to society on the part of Christians. The opportunity the Church would have to intensify its post-war activity among youth came to be uppermost in Fangen's mind. "Our people are in God's hands," he wrote to Hille, "Whatever the outcome of the war is, there will come a respite, a time of grace, perhaps the greatest opportunity for Christian work in hundreds of years."[25] Øivind Berggrav and Carl Fredrik Engelstad joined Hille and Tschudi at Dusgård to discuss with their friend the forthcoming "time of grace" for Christian work.

Illness continued to plague Fangen. He longed to visit his Swedish physician but could not, in 1942, be optimistic about his chances for doing so. During a period of good health, however, he was eager to begin writing once more. "My long novel," he wrote, "calls to me with panic in its voice!"[26]

Events of the previous two years had given Fangen time for meditation and self-examination. One aspect of his life he had carefully reconsidered was his relationship to the Oxford Group Movement. He shared his views about this relationship in a letter to Stephan Tschudi.[27] The Group had come, he explained, like John the Baptist had come before Jesus began his ministry. Buchman and his followers had preached the law and convicted him of his sin; the boldness of the Høsbjør approach had overwhelmed him. Yet the Oxford Group was guilty of prideful Pharaseeism. It had oversimplified spiritual matters, for example, by speaking of the two classes of people, "the changed and the unchanged." This weakness had now begun to disturb Fangen. He had also discovered, together with others among the "changed," that after a few months of "changed" living, one's sins began to return. It was true that the Group Movement had provided a powerful impulse which led to an "awakening," but it had not been able to provide a means for sustaining the life of faith. From his experience Fangen re-discovered the importance of the Lutheran teaching concerning the use of the Sacraments. Furthermore, he confessed:

> Early after the Group's arrival in Norway I began to have reservations about it because it gradually became clear to me that in one matter the 'gamle kristne' ('orthodox Christians') were right: a man is 'saved' by faith alone.

He asserted that the Group had neglected the proclamation of grace and the forgiveness of sins in such a way that Buchmanites had ceased being grateful for the "wonder" of this proclamation. The forgiveness of sins was

> …God's revelation of Himself. In this we live and it is only upon this we Christians can live—it is the great creative principle. When we realize this, light begins to come into the dark corners of the heart.[28]

According to Mrs. Fangen, her husband had severed his connection with the Oxford Group by 1937. That year he became very disturbed about the manner in which the Movement used his name for its publicity purposes. He decided to "resign after a speaking engagement for him was announced for which he had given no previous consent."[29] According to several of his friends, Fangen admired the organizational program of the Oxford Group Movement, but by 1937 he had become disappointed by what he considered to be its superficial theological legalism. It evaded serious discussion of current theological issues, he maintained, and for this reason he no longer received any intellectual stimulation from it.[30] In a tribute to Fredrik Ramm, a friend from early "Oxford" days, Fangen commented:

> We who were filled with assurance that we should soon experience a 'Christian world revolution' came to be bitterly disappointed. In our first great enthusiasm we had underestimated the opposition. We were Christian opti-

mists. It took time for us to become Christian realists…to live upon the minimum, namely, faith in spite of all, upon the acceptance of obedience even without results, as the missionaries have learned. We were a bit too confident in certain methods. And sooner or later, the Lord of the Church dashed this confidence to pieces. In time, all confidence in methods and in one's own pretensions is broken. This results in a humiliating crisis which reveals if we really possess faith—not in the results of our work, not in a world revolution, but if we have faith in God.[31]

In faith he learned to trust in God's power alone to "change" men's lives. "There is nothing that can make one feel so humanly powerless," he wrote, "than when he seeks to win a convert to Christian faith." He looked upon himself as merely a witness to the validity of Christian faith. He prayed that God would choose to use his life to "win" others for the Kingdom of God.[32]

But Fangen did not seek to oppose the Oxford Group publicly because he insisted it was a worthy cause if it could genuinely "change" a single person. Group methods of propaganda, however, had become distasteful to him, and privately he informed friends before 1940 that he was no longer an advocate of the religious movement.[33]

The advent of the Second World War severely disrupted the activities of the Oxford Group Movement in Norway. No public meetings were held during the years of the occupation. According to one of its leading spokesmen in Norway, Sten Bugge, the Germans were hostile to the Group Movement. Therefore, in order to sustain itself, Buchman's followers adopted a method of personal contact evangelism and avoided any attempt to choose leaders or organize houseparties.[34]

One observer maintains that the occupation caused three reactions among Group followers in Norway. The discipline of the Nazis appealed to some followers, he said, and they sympathized with the occupation forces. Other followers naively expected that the Germans could be "changed." And others, like Fangen, tried to resist them. But in order to resist as a Norwegian patriot one could not be "absolutely honest."[35]

Gradually Fangen turned his attention from the Oxford Group Movement to the Church of Norway. Here he sought and found new ties of Christian fellowship. His time in prison, especially the time in solitary confinement, had helped to teach him how necessary those ties were. And his experience with the Oxford Group had given him a lasting impression of the need for vital comradeship among Christians. He expressed this sentiment in a letter to a professor of theology, Lyder Brun, and in conversations with a bishop, Henrik Hille, who came to visit the author at Dusgård from nearby Hamar.[36]

In a letter written in 1943 Fangen expressed the hope that he might partici-pate in the work of a re-vitalized post-war Church:

> I speculate about what my role shall be when this misery of war is over. For many reasons it is well that such speculation is useless. One can see the tasks...and leave the rest in God's hand. One thing I am certain about: there will be much for Christians to do together; our task will be to have all people recognize that relevant and fruitful thoughts come from the Church which is not antagonistic to culture and to reality.[37]

He spoke to friends about creating a Christian institute in Norway patterned after the Sigtuna Foundation in Sweden.[38] This institute, as he envisioned it, would deepen and consolidate the Christian unity in Norway which had been created by the occupation. It would also seek to become a center for Norway's participation in the ecumenical movement. He hoped that the institute could begin its work soon after the war. He believed that such a development could become a means through which the Church could participate in a vital way in the post-war era of "cultural rearmament."[39]

By 1944 Fangen sensed that the war was nearing its climax. In a letter to Bjarne Hareide he wrote, "I feel the character of the war is more and more apoca-lyptic. Only God can save us from chaos, for from a human point of view there is no salvation."[40] But through a united and faithful Church God would work sal-vation. He expressed his hope for this salvation in further correspondence with Hareide. "The weakness of Norwegian Christianity," he wrote, "is that it is indi-vidualistic, preoccupied with sound doctrine, and thus unable to view the univer-sal Church with its world-wide fellowship."[41] An illustration of this weakness, to his view, was the China Mission Group's insistence upon having private com-munion services. He wrote:

> I am not a high Church man, but Norway's misfortune is having too weak a loyalty to the Church...The possibilities God has given us can be destroyed even before the peace. Then we will disappoint the people of Norway at a time when only a united Christian insight can help them in all areas of life.[42]

The China Mission Group often preferred lay preachers to ordained pastors, and this became a point of tension among Christians in Norway. Fangen claimed that the Oxford Group's work in Norway had helped to reduce tensions that had existed between clergy and laity. His broadminded view of this problem is evi-dent in his comment to Hareide:

> To be sure, we have many weak, stereotyped pastors, impressed by their education and by its terminology. But this is also true in regard to the lay preachers, and perhaps to a higher degree.... That a man should be barred from Christian fellowship <u>because</u> he is a pastor is incomprehensible to me.[43]

Illnesses associated with ulcers and gall bladder trouble sapped the author's vitality during the years of the occupation. But by 1944, he had almost completed the novel, <u>The Pastor</u> (<u>Presten</u>), and he had become a popular speaker at Christian youth meetings. In his speeches before young students, he emphasized his interpretation of the Christian view of truth, and the New Testament proclamation of the victory of Christ. These speaking engagements were high points of inspiration to Fangen. In this activity the author had fulfilled his Christian duty, as Luther saw it, "to proclaim, teach, and disseminate the Word." To Luther, the abolition of the division into clergy and laity follows as a corollary from the priesthood of all believers. Nevertheless Luther never doubted that an office of the ministry was necessary in the Church for the purpose of order in the congregation, and "that the sinner might be served with the Word of promise and forgiveness."[45] Even though he was a gifted lay preacher himself, and greatly admired the lay activity sponsored by the Oxford Group Movement, Fangen remained loyal to the Lutheran principle of a special office of an ordained ministry.

In addition to his activities as a "lay preacher," Fangen began working on a new novel having the Second World War as its background. It was based partly upon fact. In the circle of his friends in Asker, the Oslo suburb where he lived prior to moving to Dusgård in 1938, was a family which had lost a son in the war. Conrad had been impressed by the ideals of National Socialism, had volunteered in the German Army, and lost his life on the Russian front. Before his death, the young soldier wrote a number of letters to his parents from Germany and Russia in which he outlined his political philosophy. Fangen, deeply moved after having read them, declared they should be published after the war.[46]

A short time later Fangen wrote his friends and told them that Conrad's letters had so impressed him that he had gotten an idea for a novel from them: it would relate the story of two cousins, friends from childhood years, who came to be on opposite sides in their relationship to National Socialism. Working in "The Walk Toward Heaven" ("Himmelturen"), his mountain cabin near Dusgård, Fangen already had <u>An Angel of Light</u> (<u>En lysets engel</u>) well under way.[47]

During 1944 Fangen remained active as a speaker at various Church gatherings. But he wrote Harald Hille that he was "dead-tired" and bothered continually by illness. "Himmelturen," he believed, had prolonged his life.[48] As he continued his effort to write novels during these years, he described a "Christian artistry" as the perspective of his work:

> If falsifying reality hurts the Christian life, so it also hurts Christian artistry. The superficial portrayal of reality associated with the name of Christ is almost blasphemy. Where has anyone found this with Jesus, friend of publicans and sinners...? I am tempted to think that it is only Christian artistry which has both the ability and the duty to portray the world's burdens, needs and falsities in a realistic manner; only this artistry can place another reality, just as great, and much stronger, up against the world's: salvation, grace, and deliverance. Without this, the portrayal of the world's misery becomes a burden—closed, futile, and fruitless.[49]

To Fangen's view, the post-war Church in Norway would need a strong Christian daily newspaper, in the tradition of the now defunct <u>Signs of the Times</u>. There were others in the Church who had already begun to work toward this goal; as the plans for <u>Our Land</u> (<u>Vårt Land</u>) developed, Fangen joined in their efforts. Shortly before the war ended in the spring of 1945, he wrote Bjarne Hareide that the paper would soon begin publishing in Oslo. But it was not until after the occupation that he became involved with <u>Our Land</u> in a direct manner.[50]

15
CHURCH AND CULTURE

An Angel of Light appeared in the summer of 1945, shortly after the occupation ended. It describes the German occupation of Norway in its portrayal of the lives of two youths during the war years as seen through the eyes of their close relative, an Oslo pastor.

Carsten and Harald had grown up together and become fast friends. But when the World War engulfs Norway, their friendship deteriorates: on the one hand, Carsten favors German National Socialism as beneficial to Norway; on the other hand, Harald is strongly opposed to everything for which the Nazis stand. Eventually Carsten's political idealism constrains him to join the Nazi Army, and ultimately he loses his life in battle with the Russians on the Eastern Front. Harald's political idealism compels him to resist the Nazi occupation forces in Norway; ultimately he is arrested and dies in a concentration camp in Germany. This tragedy forms the structure around which Fangen develops an interpretation of St. Paul's assertion that "...even Satan disguises himself as an angel of light" (II Corinthians 11:14). According to the author's interpretation, Carsten was deceived by National Socialism disguised as an "angel of light."[51]

But the novel also gives a "picture of spiritual developments in Norway from the beginning of the nineteen-thirties through the last year of the occupation," as Carl Fredrik Engelstad has written.[52] In it Fangen insists that the Church has a strategic role to play in the continuation of Norway's spiritual development, and he warns the Church not to concentrate so much upon theological abstractions that Christian laymen lose their interest in its cause. Although the lay membership has always played a vital role in the life and mission of the Church, in An Angel of Light Fangen attempts to make this role a subject of theological reflection.

He does this by describing the struggle of the Oslo pastor to understand better his calling as a servant of the Church. The pastor has received spiritual encouragement as a result of the Oxford Group Movement's work in Norway. But as time went on he had become disillusioned: he now felt that the Group used too many clichés, that it was centered upon ethics at the expense of an eschatological perspective of man's relationship to God, and that it used the Bible in a superficial manner. The religious movement had, however, forced him to examine both his willingness and his ability to deal with the spiritual concerns of individuals. "I love the Church," he reflects, "but do I love people?" (pp. 41–49,93).

A crisis follows this disillusionment in which he considers withdrawing from the ministry. But after "sharing" his anxiety with Ellen, his wife, the pastor is converted to a "love of people." (pp. 97–101). Thereafter great numbers of people come to him for spiritual counsel. In this part of the novel Fangen underscores Cyril Eastwood's comment in regard to the "priesthood of all believers":

> All believers share a common dignity. It cannot be said that some Christians belong to a religious class and others do not. The honour and dignity conferred by Christ upon one are also conferred upon all...The Christian's calling and not his status, is the all-important fact. This calling is characterized in two distinct ways: by the possession of the grace of Christ, and by the Christian's acceptance of the role of "servant."[53]

Harald, one of the pastor's cousins portrayed in the novel, learned toward the close of his life that a Christian is called to accept the role of "servant to others." In a long letter to the pastor he admits that earlier in his life he had been unable to feel at home in the Church because it was not relevant to life. Using an Oxford Group type of cliché, Harald wrote: "I have heard many sermons about the power of sin, but not one sermon about power as sin." (p. 174). After learning about "power as sin" through his experiences in the resistance movement, Harald also learns that the Christian may express his faith by showing compassion for others: "We meet God in our neighbor," he declares (p. 347).

In Carsten's tragic death the pastor sees that "spiritual homelessness" is ultimately the result of adherence to the "angel of light," National Socialism (p. 373). He thus believes more firmly than ever that religious faith provides an avenue of redemption:

> God has given us a way out, His Kingdom of grace which exists in this world not for the purpose of fleeing from human culture, but rather for finding power to stand in culture as God Himself stood, joined with it, and dying for it. And that we might have assurance and courage, He has promised that in the fullness of time He shall make all things new and establish His everlasting Kingdom (p. 377).

Fangen never finished his next novel, <u>The Pastor</u> (<u>Presten</u>), which he intended to be the second volume of his trilogy, <u>The Mill Grinds Slowly</u> (<u>Kvernen som maler langsomt</u>).[54] In the first volume of the trilogy, <u>The Citizen's Holiday</u>, Fangen describes the milieu of Bergen in the eighteen eighties. <u>The Pastor</u> depicts the spiritual side of this same milieu in its portrayal of the life of the pastor, Henrik

Holter. The novel includes many religious discussions which add nothing new to the religious views the author expresses in the other novels he wrote after 1934. These discussions lack an organic connection to the plot and indicates that possibly the author had intended to work through the material again before its publication.

Fangen concentrated his thoughts in a better fashion in the essays, sermons, and articles he wrote during the months between the end of the occupation and his death in 1946. In them he probed the tension involved in the relationship between the Church and the society in which it exists. Of particular importance in this connection is the essay, "The Problem of Culture" ("Kulturproblemet") written in reply to an essay by Ole Hallesby, "Our Pietistic Line" ("Vår pietistiske linje").[55]

Hallesby's essay discusses the tension between Church and culture in terms of a "Christ against culture" position.[56] Upon the basis of the Bible, Church history, and the Lutheran confessions, Hallesby denounces what he terms the "secularization of Norway's culture," and he calls for an "awakening" among both Christians and non-Christians. Writing nine months after the liberation of Norway, he maintains that Norway had not yet begun its anticipated "spiritual rebirth."

In his reply, Fangen acknowledges his admiration for Hallesby's "experience and compassion"; he agrees that the post-war "spiritual rebirth" had not arrived. But he insists that Hallesby's "Christ against culture" position is an over-simplification of the problem because "Christian faith concerns the whole man and everything in human life." If the Christian religion is "over-simplified into moralism," and from a negative stance "denies" culture, then it becomes so removed from men's experience that they may be tempted to follow political totalitarian powers. Thus it is necessary for all Christians to assume a positive stance in regard to man's cultural life; the question concerning how this should be done is another matter. "But above all," he wrote, "entry into the world of faith must not be closed by the prohibition of adiaphora...."[57]

Fangen cites the example of Jesus, who attended the wedding at Cana, and was known as the "friend of publicans and sinners." (John 2:1–11, Matthew 11:19). He declares,

> I believe Christ would condemn with strong words a proclamation of Christianity which elevates outward prohibitions as qualifications for entrance to God's Kingdom, and the criteria of living faith.[58]

Fangen reminds his readers that, according to the New Testament writers, Christ brought a new order to the world, the beginning of a new aeon. Therefore, "...moralistic and dogmatic degrading of the Gospel into the commonplace removes from its cosmic perspective and bearing." At the same time he warns that an emphasis upon Christian eschatology may also degrade the Gospel by refusing to take seriously its relevance to man's culture. Fangen saw the solution to the problem of culture in a theological renascence "which recognizes and builds upon the universality of Christianity."[59]

The seriousness with which the author viewed the problem of human sin restrained him from advocating that Christianity might become a religion of moral training which would work toward the establishment of a peaceful, co-operative society. This is one reason why he did not publicly endorse the Moral Re-Armament phase of the Oxford Group Movement. Rather, he sought to deal with the tension resulting from the Church's relationship to culture with a "both-and" response by accepting the paradoxes involved in the relationship. He insists that Christians remain loyal to Christ while at the same time they participate in man's cultural activity. Fangen could never join hands with the Christian who would reject culture in pronouncing the whole world of human culture to be godless for one cannot escape from the world which God created and sustains. Hence he dealt with paradoxes in his writings; he stood on the side of men in the encounter with God, yet sought also to interpret the word of God which he heard from "the other side." He learned how the Christian must live in the tension between revelation and reason and between being under the law of God while yet being under God's grace. He knew Christ by experience and yet he walked by faith. But he also recognized that as long as life lasts there is sin; hence, there would be no solution of the dilemma this side of death. Living between time and eternity, wrath and mercy, between Christ and culture he maintained that the Christian inevitably finds life both tragic and joyful. The character of the pastor in An Angel of Light vividly portrays this vision.

Fangen's post-Høsbjør novels attempt to depict the shallow-ness, the futility, and the meaninglessness of a materialistic life. In seeking to remain both intellectually honest and sincerely devout, he expressed an intense desire that the Church, instead of withdrawing from the world of culture, should appreciate and learn from the arts, which to him were a reflection of man himself. In the arts we see how the thought and expression of man change in succeeding generations. He was concerned lest the Church become so self-centered in developing its own categories of expression, understood only by those on the "inside," that its dialogue with the world would be broken off. He realized that the Church could neither accommodate its message to every change of man nor lack an awareness of up-to-date cultural moods, because the communication of its proclamation was at stake. There is a constant tension to communicate in the best way the message of the Church in each generation; with this tension Fangen wrestled.

5

CHILDREN OF LIGHT

○ ○

O Day full of grace which we behold,
Now gently to view ascending;
Thou over the earth thy reign unfold,
Good cheer to all mortals lending:
That children of light in every clime
May prove that the night is ending.

—N. F. S. Grundtvig, 1826

79

16
THE KINGDOM OF GRACE

"Through all his years," writes Carl Fredrik Engelstad, "Fangen was occupied with—yes, one is tempted to say possessed by—thoughts concerning the kingdom of God…"[1] The Kingdom of Grace (Nåderiket) is a collection of addresses Fangen delivered at Christian student meetings and Church worship services during the years of the occupation. Carl Fredrik Engelstad edited the book after Fangen's death in 1946.

The Kingdom of Grace reveals the author's keen interest in biblical theology. For not only does the topic of the "kingdom" loom large in the teachings of Jesus; it is to be found also, in one form or another, through the length and breadth of the Bible.[2] Although Fangen's writings from the time before his association with the Oxford Group Movement are marked by an occasional biblical quotation, in none of them is the author so concerned with biblical theology. There is a quality of joy and confidence in The Kingdom of Grace. Here Fangen proclaims his loyalty to the Christian gospel; he discusses the Christian life but avoids using any Oxford Group moral exhortations in doing so. The sermons of The Kingdom of Grace are related to the quality of preaching which is found in the New Testament, where preaching the gospel is not the same thing as delivering moral exhortation. Although the early Church was occupied in teaching the knowledge of its Lord, it did not make converts by teaching; rather, it was by "kerygma" ("proclamation"), says St. Paul, not "didache" ("teaching") that it "pleased God to save men."[3]

According to Fangen, the sphere of the kingdom of Christ includes all men:

> Christ invites and receives us as sick and sinful human beings who are neither good nor heroic. That the kingdom of grace, is for all men is a mystery…The decisive element of life is that God in Jesus Christ identified himself with all of mankind (pp. 20, 24).

The mission of the kingdom of Christ is described not in terms of Oxford Group directives, but rather in terms of biblical theology:

God's grace is creative…for in it He does not evaluate us in terms of our individualism, but in terms of our participation in the communion of saints, with Christ, who came not to judge the world but to save it. Christ has broken the dominion of sin so that we, in the midst of a sinful world, may struggle against the dominion of sin in Christ's power (p. 218).

In 1947 Carl Fredrik Engelstad edited another collection of Fangen's essays which he entitled, Concerning Freedom (Om frihet).[4] It contains several sermons similar to those found in The Kingdom of Grace, the essay, "Concerning Faithfulness," and several essays Fangen contributed to the Swedish periodical, Bonniers Literary Magazine.

In the fall of 1943 Fangen wrote to one of his friends, "I love fall for the clearness and peace it brings to the countryside. And I ponder this fall's world-shaking history with prayerful longing: 'Amen. Come, Lord Jesus.' As far as death is concerned, I am uncertain. Yet the assurance that 'here we have no abiding place' and that 'our citizenship is in heaven' grows stronger and stronger in me. I would be happy to depart and to be with Christ. In other words, I do not believe in any death. I believe as the early Christians did, that our time of death is our true birth unto life." [5]

The religious views he expresses in Concerning Freedom, The Kingdom of Grace, and other writings from this period reflect this emphasis upon eschatology and the consummation of the kingdom of Christ. In 1945 he wrote:

Reading about Hiroshima and the A-bomb is like reading a chapter from Revelation; it is an apocalyptic symbol. To betray our essential identity as men of faith is the same thing as suicide…Truth, righteousness, and love are the powers of eternity…[6]

Soon after the occupation ended in 1945, a new Christian newspaper, Our Land (Vårt Land), began publishing in Oslo. Fangen hoped in vain that it might become the successor to the defunct Signs of the Times. This disappointment stemmed from his disagreement with the newspaper's advertising policy.[7] Conservative elements among those who supported the paper, led by Ole Hallesby, proposed to editor Bjarne Høye that movie and theatre advertisements be deleted from the paper in order to "save" it.[8]

At a meeting of Our Land's Board of Directors on January 9, 1946, Fangen objected to this proposition. He argued:

> I deplore the moral ideals being proclaimed to youth today, for my having had much to do with the Oxford Group's work has not been without effect. But the Christian life is a fruit of faith and it is a secondary matter that a man keeps away from tobacco, and so forth, in order to keep from becoming a bitter enemy of Jesus Christ. We must not confuse Christianity with moralism.[9]

Maintaining that Christians in Norway should take a positive stance in relation to culture, Fangen insisted that films and dramas might give Christians the opportunity to influence culture. At the same time, he sought to reconcile those among Our Land's supporters who either supported or opposed his point of view. He also thought that the newspaper might become the organ of the newly formed "Christian People's Party" ("Kristelig folkeparti").[11] Fangen's unsuccessful effort to influence the policy in regard to movie and theatre advertisements during the early months of Our Land's existence had its basis in that element of his Christian humanism which held that all Christian doctrine must be continually viewed in relation to human experience.

In the closing months of his life Fangen challenged Christians in Norway to unite their efforts, to participate in political affairs, and thereby witness that the Christian religion was relevant to all areas of life.[12] He insisted that his emerging vision of the Church as "the kingdom of Christ" was based upon orthodox Christianity. To Stephan Tschudi he wrote:

> I am what we call orthodox. In any event, my faith in the divinity of Christ is rock solid. All attempts to humanize God and make his revelation and work of salvation acceptable for flesh and blood's understanding is essentially blasphemous. As you know, divinely revealed forgiveness and the relationship between sin and grace is for me a decisive proof of God.[13]

The Christian life, as Fangen saw it, was not a matter of dogma alone; it also involved an attitude, a perspective, a method of life. It was this conviction, tested by his clear intellect, but somehow obscured by his lively imagination perhaps, which has provided the basis for his genuine contribution to twentieth century church life in Norway.

In the spring of 1946 when the condition of Fangen's health grew worse, he decided to seek medical attention in Sweden. Although he hesitated in deciding to journey so far, he wrote to a friend, "If one can fly, travel is not so bad."[14] Fangen cancelled his flight reservation for May 20, however, in order to attend the meeting of Our Land's editorial board on that day. When Sten Bugge happened to meet him on May 21, Fangen explained the reason for the delay and added, "I want to see this matter through."[15]

Arne Fjelberg left the Our Land meeting with Fangen. He related that as they walked together along the Palace Park in Oslo, Fangen asked him to take his place at a forthcoming lecture he was to deliver, and said, "I am longing for heaven!" Fjelberg's impression was that Fangen was very depressed, and he gathered from their conversation that he believed his life's work was completed.

The following day Fangen arrived at Fornebu Airport in Oslo. He telephoned Odd Eidem, a young writer friend, to tell him that he would read a copy of his new play on the flight to Stockholm.[17] The aircraft Fangen boarded had been obtained from the Germans following the occupation, and was a tri-motored transport of the Junkers Ju-52 type. He took his place at seat seven, on the port side. In front of him sat the wife of Isaac Grünewald, the Swedish painter. Across the aisle sat a businessman, Hans Kiaer. Other passengers included the jurist, Adolf Lindvik, and there was a crew of three.

Hans Kiaer recalled that the take-off at 12:45 p.m. was normal. When the aircraft began to bank leftward at approximately a thirty-degree angle, he glanced at Fangen and noticed his apprehension. Kiaer smiled in attempting to reassure Fangen, because Kiaer had flown in a Ju-52 before and he thought the turn was part of the normal procedure on a flight to Stockholm. He heard nothing unusual about the sound of the motors, but suddenly he saw the left wing knife into some birch trees. A tremendous crash followed.

The aircraft had fallen between two houses on Halden Terrasse, adjacent to the Airport. Kiaer, the only survivor, emerged from a hole in the side of the aircraft and rolled away from the wreckage which began to burn fiercely. Kiaer recalled that he never lost consciousness and he believes this circumstance saved his life.[19] News of the accident came as a great shock to the Norwegian public, and an Investigation Commission was formed to try to determine its cause.[20]

Hundreds of persons could not find room in Our Savior's, the Cathedral Church of Oslo, where funeral services for Fangen were held in the morning of May 27. Final rites began with a reading of the author's poem "Passion," a meditation upon the death of Christ. The "Arioso and Choir" section of his Mission Cantata and the Brorson hymn "I See Thee Lamb of God" were sung.

Bishop Berggrav spoke and used Psalm 121 as a text. Fangen, he said, "was a lover of life, a realist who stood in this world, but above all else was a lover of eternity. There he discovered steadfast reality." Bishop Hille and a friend, Arne Fjelberg, spoke at the graveside services held later that afternoon near Hamar.[21]

The spring sunshine added a benediction when Ronald Fangen was laid to rest in the Ringsaker Churchyard near his beloved Dusgård.

17
A "CHRISTIAN HUMANIST"

In response to a review of Fangen's book <u>Christianity and Our Time</u>, by Professor Lyder Brun, Fangen described himself as a "Christian humanist."[22] In his essays, dramas and novels, Fangen revealed himself as one who respected man's spiritual life; in this sense he was a "humanist." He did not believe, however, that man's capacities for good were without limitation. While acknowledging the good in man, he recognized his evil nature as well. He urged that the only way to balance these destructive forces and resolve man's predicament was to bring him within the sphere of the Christian proclamation. Fangen was thus also a "Christian," for he believed in the Christian doctrine of sin; man is imperfect and limited but responsible for his acts. Man was bound to nature and its laws but not to be explained by them. He was not only a product of biological, economic and social conditions, but was also a person, created in the "image of God," who struggled with the inner forces of conscience and will. A scientific analysis of man as part of nature was not necessarily false; it was only a secondary part of the truth about him, and therefore incomplete. Man was primarily a spiritual being, created for communion with God.

"Humanism" is a concern to understand and to change the world so that human life becomes more valuable to more people. The heritage of humanism is usually associated with the literary humanism related to the European rediscovery of Greek and Latin literature at the time of the Renaissance. The "humanists" were the scholars who devoted themselves to these studies. Hence the term "humanities" has been used in the universities for the arts and the non-scientific subjects.

Modern humanism, as distinguished from literary and religious humanism, cultivates an attitude of mind, illustrated best perhaps by Julian Huxley and Jean-Paul Sartre, that man is "alone" and that he alone is responsible for himself and his fellow men. Trusting in reason and the "open mind," this attitude undergirds an effort to create a more free and open society.

Nothing human could be foreign to Ronald Fangen's interest, yet when he described himself as a "Christian" humanist he attempted to avoid the danger of making humanism, as described above, an alternative to Christian faith. Rather than becoming preoccupied with individual salvation or an eschatological, otherworldly focus of interest, Fangen sought, especially in his later writings, to give full value to human life in this world and allow it relative autonomy. This was possible because of his belief that ultimately the world was God's and that man lived in a God-given autonomy.

If humanism is said to proceed from the assumption that man is "on his own" and this life is all, then no Christian is a humanist in that sense. Humanism, after all, may only exist in the personal thought and lives of those who by their example promote a certain humanistic posture, and not any philosophy of humanism.

Fangen's humanism is known best by the many distinguished friends he inspired before his untimely death.[23] A number of basic ideas, however, often alluded to and reflected upon in his writings, reveal the general content of his Christian humanism. First of all, he opposed any humanism which did not retain the religious categories of the sacred, the holy, the worshipful, the eternal, and the absolute. Human pride could not be enthroned. Any humanist assumption that the world and human life are products of chance, that man and his environment are doomed to ultimate extinction, that there is no justification for it all, no purpose, was to his view both incredible and intolerable.

Secondly, humanism which depends upon man "on his own" becomes too rational. Fangen's conviction, illustrated best by Klaus Hallem in Duel, held that most persons do not live rationally. Such humanism therefore errs by counting too much on reason, and also by its neglect of deep emotional and imaginative needs. In the final analysis man's unconquerable enemy may be himself; man is doomed by an inner contradiction-described by the mysterious doctrine of sin-which abounds in human life and for which humanism offers no remedy. Gottfried Stein in The Man Who Loved Righteousness learns this in the final tragic circumstances of his life. For Fangen, man's inhumanity to man, the track of evil brought by violence springing from envy, pride, and sensual passion was very real; how to bring this human inheritance under control in ourselves and in the world is a most persistent question. Olaf Årvik in Fall into Sin is a literary portrait of this struggle. The human condition involves total dependence. Fall into Sin is an invitation to repent, not argue, and to trust.

Another basic aspect of the author's Christian humanism was his awareness of Western historical traditions. His book reviews and essays (for example, Christianity and Our Time) reveal a keen appreciation for Western culture. The humane and enlightened Christianity of an Erasmus and a Thomas More illustrate the power of the tradition of Christian humanism his work represents. Augustine, Melanchthon, John Milton, and T. S. Eliot are also in the line of those who dedicated themselves to a disciplined concern for the relations between traditional Christianity and humane culture. Fangen sought to re-establish the claims of such a humanism in our time.

In the fourth place, a humanism which left man completely "on his own" belies its name because it neglects the aspirations of the human spirit. Humanists of the past have tended to be one-sided; the rationalists (scientific humanism) the moralists (ethical humanism), and the secularists (secular humanism) represent the danger of reducing man to a physical organism. Erik Hamre in the novel Erik is one who aspires to fuller spiritual dimensions of life. Christian faith was the reward of his quest.

Lastly, basic to Fangen's Christian humanism was his eager desire to transmit this value to the coming generation. His popularity as a speaker before youth gatherings, especially during the post-Høsbjør years, testifies to this. The success which greeted his efforts to inspire young people is evident in the tributes written in the journal Church and Culture in commemoration of his seventieth birthday anniversary.[24] Fangen held that Christian faith was the supreme value parents might give their children in an age of rootlessness and drift. Without this faith and hope, life becomes shallow and superficial. T. S. Eliot's poem The Hollow Men opens, with a graphic summary of such secularism in full bloom:

> We are the hollow men
> We are the stuffed men
> Leaning together
> Headpiece filled with straw. Alas!
> Our dried voices, when
> We whisper together
> Are quiet and meaningless
> As wind in dry grass
> Or rats' feet over broken glass
> In our dry cellar.
>
> Shape without form, shade without colour,
> Paralyzed force, gesture without motion;
> Those who have crossed
> With direct eyes, to death's other Kingdom
> Remember us-if at all-not as lost
> Violent souls, but only
> As the hollow men
> The stuffed men.[25]

Fangen's Christian interpretation of life filled him with peace in the midst of conflict, and joy in the dedicated effort he made to make Christian faith more intelligible and credible to modern "secular" man.

18
LITERATURE AND THE CHRISTIAN LIFE

The Church in America had entered the decade of the seventies in virtually a crisis atmosphere. With the postwar boom of the forties and fifties long ended, unrest and turbulence are facts of life in most major religious bodies. Membership is becoming increasingly polarized between black and white, old and young, layman and clergyman, activist and pietist. Some church bodies are faced with a shortage of clergymen and it is becoming increasingly difficult to recruit seminary students. Of those students who are ordained, the number who resign is rising. Missionary work at home and abroad faces new and complex difficulties. Church related educational institutions report financial straits. Cutbacks and belt-tightening are reported almost all along the way in denominational circles.

Behind the crisis atmosphere were such far-reaching questions as these; On the one hand, in what manner may the Church become more actively involved in social, political, and economic issues? On the other hand, should the Church tone down such involvement and concentrate upon "saving souls?" How is the Christian Gospel related to the war on pollution and poverty, urban renewal, amnesty and "women's lib"?

The writer maintains that one way to deal seriously with such questions as these is to learn more about their cultural backgrounds. For this purpose the twentieth century writer may be given a more attentive hearing. In this connection one might think immediately of such novelists as Graham Green and William Golding in Great Britain, and John Updike in our country. In Scandinavia Kaj Munk, Sigrid Undset, and Olōv Hartman come to mind. Although he did not reach the literary achievement of these writers, Ronald Fangen's work makes a worthy contribution to the growing interest in the dialogue concerning relationships between Christian theology and literature. These relationships are often ignored, especially in Lutheran Church circles. Yet in a letter he wrote in 1523, Martin Luther analyzed the relationship between Christianity and literary culture in this manner:

> I am persuaded that without knowledge of literature, pure theology cannot at all endure, just as heretofore, when letters have declined and lain prostrate, theology, too, has wretchedly fallen and lain prostrate; nay I see that there has never been a great revelation of the Word of God unless He has first prepared the way by the rise and prosperity of languages and letters, as though they were John the Baptists. Certainly it is my desire that there shall be as many

> poets and rhetoricians as possible, because I see that by these studies, as by no other means, people are wonderfully fitted for the grasping of sacred truth and for handling it skillfully and happily. Therefore I beg of you that at my request (if that has any weight) you will urge your young people to be diligent in the study of poetry and rhetoric.[26]

The dialogue between a given writer and Christian faith is distorted, however, if the "Christian perspective" is used as a kind of yardstick by which to measure the writer's religious stature and then render judgment upon it. Instead, one may use this perspective as a means of getting at the nature of a writer's commitment, as a way of coming to terms with the religious seriousness and importance of his work, whatever the nature of his faith may be. A Christian should seek to enter into conversation with the writer but not at the expense of the writer's art or his integrity as a person. With Fangen's literary works the task of entering into such conversation is complex (especially for the foreign reader) but it is made easier because of the frequent "open" stance this author takes in reference to Christianity and the Lutheran Church in particular.

For the Christian reader, the dialogue with contemporary literature offers the challenge of encounter with the world in which he lives and to which he speaks. This literature gives him an opportunity to view his surroundings with the powerful clarity of vision that the imaginative writer can alone bring to it. In this encounter, the Christian can find the sort of self-understanding—both as a person and as a Christian—that results when one participates in and serves this world rather than fleeing from it in condemnation and fear. He will participate in the atmosphere that the contemporary writer depicts not only because he listens attentively to it, but also because he recognizes that the artist's image of man-however tortured or despairing it may be-is also the image of the kind of men who attempt to be Christian. The demonic image which we often behold in the literary looking glass has features that belong to us all, and no one who, in repentance, acknowledges his identity with the world dare deny this. Thus, the contemporary writer's effort may also contribute to our self-definition as Christians, not because it is a reflection of a world in which we are condemned to live, but because it is the world into which we have been sent as disciples and servants. By acknowledging our participation in the world as Christ's followers, we will come to understand more about what its redemption means and what it costs. The noted critic Nathan A. Scott, Jr. in his The Broken Center: Studies in the Theological Horizon of Modern Literature offers a profound exploration of the constructive possibilities for dialogue between theology and literature.

Roland Frye has pointed out that literature may be related to Christian tradition in three ways: first, as literary method in the use of symbol, metaphor, and story as applicable to the understanding of the Biblical message; second, as literature treats, in universal terms, both the affirmations and the problems of human existence with which Christian theology must come to grips; and last, as specific writers express their visions of life in terms of a Christian frame of reference.[27] Erik, Duel, and The Man Who Loved Righteousness are illustrations of Fangen's contribution to the second of Frye's contentions, and an essay collection such as Christianity and Our Time is an illustration of the third relationship.

One of the themes of the Bible is the story of the people of God. The Church, considered as the people of God today, is a realm of His continued activity. The Church's sacraments of baptism and the Lord's Supper demonstrate God's individualized grace and at the same time initiate the Christian into a community of faith. Together with others in this fellowship, he experiences renewal and celebrates the gift of freedom in Christ. Ultimately, therefore, the Christian cannot escape the Church. Such was the case with Ronald Fangen who was a churchman all his life. Nurtured in faith by the Church of Norway's ministry of the word and sacrament, he rejoiced in the life of faith which flowed out from this ministry. Yet he also championed Christian individual diversity of experience and expression as belonging to the freedom of the Gospel. This tension is frequently reflected in his writings.

The American religious scene is larger and more complex than the Norwegian. The issues of the nineties—poverty, ecology, and sexuality in particular—have greater depth and urgency in our country. Criticisms of "the establishment" continue and accelerate. By comparison, one may observe complex differences between the Norwegian background of the "state church" and the American context of "religious pluralism." Geographical differences, however, are becoming a diminishing barrier toward understanding these backgrounds. Exchanges of tourists to both countries has become commonplace. We live in a world where cultural borderlines are rapidly disappearing, and where Christian cultural provincialism is doomed. Thus, prejudices formed across the Atlantic in past decades are fading; today's religious concerns are scarcely limited by geographical factors. The surge to power by the "Third World" is evident, and latent concern for the very survival of our planet haunts Christian and non-Christian alike.

"Where there is no vision" a biblical writer reminds us, "the people perish" (Prov. 29:18, KJV). Ronald Fangen, a writer and layman of the Church of Norway, had a vision of new possibilities for new life in the Church of the twentieth century. He was "ahead of his time"; in Christian freedom he looked upon Christ as Lord over both society with its structures and the individual believer as well. As a literary artist he appealed to the education of the reader's sensibility to the truth of human experience. Although literature is not at the heart of Christian life, that moment of trust in God's mercy and love, it is perpetually relevant to the Christian view of life because it educates man's special powers of insight and compassion to the richness of human life-its paradoxical, wayward, and imperfect nature included-and forces one out of old patterns of response to the world around us.

Although Fangen did not live to experience the tumults of change which have occurred already in this second half of the twentieth century, his prophetic vision applauded the value of the involvement of the Church in "worldly" concerns. His Christian humanism, though deeply moved by the art, music, and theology of the Church, nevertheless led him to criticize the Church for its short-sighted social awareness. Love for Church tradition and practice could not stand in the way of his urgent counsel for the Lutheran Church to become something more in the total affairs of modern man. Above all groupings, Fangen set the community of Jesus Christ, the Church Universal. For him, Christian unity was not something Christ's followers achieve for their master; rather it is something Christians have.

This pioneer, let it not be overlooked, was a layman. His life is a token of that vital role which laymen have played in the Christian Church through the centuries; at the same time, it is a foretaste of the fruits of the increasing responsibility which laypersons must assume in the Church of today and tomorrow.

NOTES

NOTES

Chapter One

[1]Review of The Weak (De svake), Oslo Dagbladet, August 23, 1920.

[2]Sambaandet, July 22, 1911, p. 2.

[3]Ibid., Feb. 17 and March 12, 1912.

[4]Handwritten copy, Carl Fredrik Engelstad.

[5]Interview with Henrik Groth, December 20, 1957.

[6]Interview with Solveig Fangen, April 23, 1961; Oslo Daily News (Dagbladet), October 23, 1920; Oslo Signs of the Times (Tidens Tegn), October 27, 1920.

[7]Page references are taken from vol. IX of the Gyldendal Norsk Forlag edition of the author's Collected Works (Samlede verker, 9 vol., 1948).

[8]Halvdan Koht and Sigmund Skard, The Voice of Norway (New York: Columbia University Press, 1944), pp. 88–89.

[9]Ibid., pp. 92–93.

[10]Wilhelm Keilhau, Det norske folks liv og historie i vår egen tid (Oslo: Askehoug, 1938), p. 210. For a full account of social legislation see pp. 203–217.

[11]Frede Castberg, The Norwegian Way of Life (London: William Heinemann Ltd., 1954), pp. 67–68.

[12]Koht and Skard, op. cit., pp. 102–109.

[13]Editorial, Vor Verden (Sept. 23, 1924), 1-2.

[14]Editorial, Vor Verden (Sept. 15, 1923), 1–2.

[15]"Kommunist Kjønsmoral," Tidens Tegn, June 17, 1923, p.5

[16]Editorial, Vor Verden (March 15, 1926), 186–187.

[17]Kristian Elster, Illustrert Norsk litteratur historie, vol. VI (Oslo: Gyldendal, 1934), p. 127.

[18]Keilhau, op. cit., pp. 408–440.

[19]Trygve Bull, Mot Dag og Erling Falk (Oslo: Cappelen, 1955), p. 55.

[20]Editorial, Mot Dag (Sept. 10, 1921), 1–2.

[21]Bull, op. cit., pp. 33–35.

[22]Editorial, Vor Verden (Aug. 1, 1938), 145.

[23]Charles Kent et al., Skillelinjen (Oslo: Gyldendal, 1931).

[24]See Alex Johnson, Eivind Berggrav: Man of the Hour (Spenningens mann) Oslo: Land og Kirke, 1959.

[25]Tidens Tegn, Oct. 3, 1928. Here Fangen reviews Berggrav's The Soul of the Prisoner Compared With Ours (Fangens sjel og vor egen).

[26]Ibid., Dec. 9, 1929.

[27] RF: A Man and His Times (En mann og hans samtid) Oslo: Gyldendal, 1946, p. 69.

[28]Signs and Deeds (Tegn og gjaerninger) Oslo: Gyldendal, 1927; Tidens Tegn, May 3, 1926.

[29]Collected Works, vol. I, pp. 59–82.

[30]Keilhau, op cit., p. 185.

[31]Collected Works, vol. I, p. 154.

[32]Knut Jarl, Edda XXXIII (October, 1931), 179–191; Johannes Lavik, The Day (Dagen), Nov. 14, 1931.

[33]June 25, 1934. Trans. Paula Wiking. (New York: Viking Press, 1934).

[34]Collected Works, vol. III

[35]Ibid., vol. IV; Interview with Solveig Fangen (June. 10, 1958).

[36]Signs of the Times, April 9, 1932.

[37]Ibid., "Church and Synagogue," June 11, 1934.

[38]Oslo Daily News, August 18, 1934.

NOTES

Chapter Two

[1]Recent promotional methods include the magazine Pace, marketed on new-stands, and the "Up With People" telecasts and campus presentations (Christianity Today, September 16, 1966, p. 30, and Calvin Trillin, "U.S. Letter: Chicago", The New Yorker, December 16, 1967, pp. 128–137). For discussions of MRA cf. Time, October 30, 1964, p. 74; New York Times, February 26, 1965 (Peter Howard obituary), Martin E. Marty, "MRA: The New Druseanism," Christian Century, March 31, 1965, pp. 399–401. Peter Howard's Frank Buchman's Secret (Garden City, N.Y.: Doubleday and Co., 1961) is a tribute to the late founder of MRA written by one of his followers.

[2]Tom Driberg, The Mystery of Moral Re-Armament (London: Secker and Warburg, 1964), p. 18.

[3]Walter H. Clark, The Oxford Group (New York: Bookman Associates, Inc., 1951), pp. 118–120.

[4]Kerr D. Macmillan, Protestantism in Germany (London: Oxford University Press, 1917), pp. 130–163 239.

[5]William Sweet, The Story of Religion in America (New York: Harper and Brothers, 1930), pp. 106–114; 116.

[6]Clark, loc. cit.

[7]Theodore G. Tappert, History of the Lutheran Theological Seminary at Philadelphia 1864–1964 (Philadelphia: Lutheran Theological Seminary, 1964), pp. 69–74.

[8]Sweet, op. cit., p. 423; Allan W. Eister, Drawing-Room Conversion (Durham: Duke University Press, 1950), pp. 29–31.

[9]A.J. Russell, For Sinners Only (London: Hodder and Stoughton, Ltd., 1932), pp. 57–58.

[10] Ibid., p. 59.

[11]Henry P. Van Dusen, "Apostle to the Twentieth Century," The Atlantic Monthly, vol. 154 (July, 1934), p. 5.

[12]Clark, op. cit., pp. 15–17; 46–52.

[13]Frank N.D. Buchman, Remaking the World (New York: Robert M. McBride and Company, 1949), p. 32.

[14]Van Dusen, loc. cit.

[15]Eister, op. cit., p. 24.

[16]Kenneth Brown, "A Religious House-Party," Outlook, vol. 139 (January, 1925), 27–28.

[17]Van Dusen, loc. cit. A full account of the Princeton episode may be found in Clark, op. cit., pp. 67–74.

[18]R.H.S. Crossman, (ed.), Oxford and the Groups (London: Basil Blackwell, 1934), pp. 12–18.

[19]Driberg, op. cit., p. 52. The name has caused confusion because the religious movement which began in the Church of England in 1833 is known as the Oxford Movement. For a description of this movement see S.L. Ollard, A Short History of the Oxford Movement (London: A.R. Mowbray and Co., 1915). The term "Group" will be used as an abbreviation for the name "Oxford Group Movement."

[20]Buchman, loc. cit.

[21]Committee of Thirty, The Challenge of the Oxford Group Movement (Toronto: The Ryerson Press, 1933; pam., 32 pp.), PP. 4–7.

[22]Buchman, op. cit., p. 78.

[23]V.C. Kitchen, I Was a Pagan (New York: Harper and Brothers, 1934).

[24]Emil Brunner, The Church and the Oxford Group, trans. David Cairns (London: Hodder and Stoughton, 1937). Samuel Shoemaker, The Church and the Oxford Group (n.n., 1933; pam., 10 pp.).

[25]Brunner, op. cit., p. 106.

[26]Shoemaker, op. cit., pp. 6–7.

[27]Buchman, op. cit., p. 42.

[28]Julian P. Thornton-Duesbury, The Oxford Group (London: Hazell, Watson and Viney, Ltd., 1947; pam. 27 pp.), p. 9.

[29]Laymen With a Notebook (foreword by L.W. Grensted), What Is the Oxford Group? (New York: Oxford University Press, 1933), pp. 67–72; Eleanor Forde, op. cit., pp. 19–28.

[30]A.J. Russell, For Sinners Only (London: Hodder and Stoughton, 1932), p. 230. For examples of guidance see the chapter "How God Guides" in his book, One Thing I Know (New York: Harper and Brothers, 1933), pp. 230–252. Cecil Rose, Wenn der Menseh Horcht (Zurich: Gotthelf Verlag, 1946) is a commentary upon Buchman's saying, "If man listens, God speaks; if man obeys, God acts," p. 72.

[31]Henry P. Van Dusen, "The Oxford Group Movement," Atlantic Monthly, vol. 154 (August, 1934), 248.

[32]Sherwood Day, The Principles of the Group (Oxford: Oxford University Press, 1934; pam., 11 pp.), pp. 1-2.

[33]Cyril Bardsley, et al., "Stories of our Oxford House Party," reprinted from The Church of England Newspaper, July 17, 1931.

[34]Harold Begbie, More Twice-Born Men (New York: G.P. Putnam's Sons, 1923), pp. 32–34.

[35]Kenneth Latourette, The Twentieth Century Outside Europe, vol. V of Christianity in a Revolutionary Age, A History of Christianity in the Nineteenth and Twentieth Centuries (New York: Harper and Row, 1962), pp. 61–63.

[36]Peter Howard, That Man Frank Buchman (London: Bland-ford Press, 1946), pp. 14–15.

[37]Peter Howard, That Man Frank Buchman (London: Bland-ford Press, 1946), p. 15; Buchman, op. cit., p. 16.

[38]Letter, Feb. 1, 1961.

[39]Oxfordbevegelsen i Norge, Articler, referater og intervujer (Oslo: Blix forlag, 1935), I, 81; II, 15; Oslo Morgenposten. Oct. 27 and Nov. 6, 1934; Oslo Aftenposten, No. 559, Nov. 5, 1934, No. 547, Oct. 29, 1934; No. 559, Nov. 5, 1934.

[40]Interview, Oct. 4, 1957.

[41]J.M. Wisløff, For fattig og rik, Nov. 18, 1934 p. 3.

[42]Interview with Randulf Haslund, July 18, 1961. Haslund stated he became Norway's first full time Group worker in 1934.

[43]En kristen verdensrevolusjon, (Oslo: Gyldendal, 1935), pp. 14–16.

[44]Letter, July 8, 1961.

[45]Interview, Nov. 14, 1957.

[46]Oslo Dagbladet, Nov. 8, 1934.

[47]Oslo Arbeiderbladet, Oct. 26, 1934.

[48]Oslo Aftenposten, No. 542, Oct. 26; No. 547, Oct. 29; No. 559, Nov. 5; No. 585, Nov. 8, 1934; Oslo Dagbladet, Nov. 13, 1934. See also Oxfordbevegelsen i Norge, op. cit., vol. I.

[49]Nov. 9, 1934.

[50]Tidens Tegn, Nov. 9, 1934.

[51]Interviews, March 10 and April 23, 1961.

[52]Oslo Aftenposten, Morgenposten, Nov. 9 and 12, 1934.

[53]Interview with Alex Johnson, Jan. 8, 1958. See also Oslo Aftenposten and Tidens Tegn, Nov. 14, 1934.

[54]Oslo Aftenposten, Nov. 15, 1934.

[55]Oxfordbevegelsen i Norge, op. cit., pp. 20–21.

[56]Arne Stai, Norsk kultur og moraldebatt i 1930 årene (Oslo: Gyldendal, 1954), p. 28.

[57]Oslo <u>Aftenposten</u>, Nov. 26, 1934; <u>Oxfordbevegelsen i Norge</u>, <u>op</u>. <u>cit</u>., I, pp. 142–145.

[58]Bergen <u>Morgenavisen</u>, Dec. 5, 1934; <u>Oxfordbevegelsen i Norge</u>, <u>op</u>. <u>cit</u>., II, pp. 141–147. Trondheim <u>Dagsposten</u>, Nov. 20 and 21, 1934.

[59]Oslo <u>Tidens Tegn</u>, May 20, 1935; Copenhagen <u>Berlinske Tidende</u>, May 23, 1946. Larvik <u>Østlands-Posten</u>, August 12, 1935.

[60]Oslo <u>Tidens Tegn</u>, Sept. 2, 1935. Oslo <u>Nationen</u>, Sept. 3, 1935.

[61]Tromsø <u>Stiftstidende</u>, August 22 and 23, 1935. In an interview on Oct. 23, 1957, Sten Bugge declared Berggrav had invited the team to Tromsø.

[62]Page 10. Alex Johnson in Peter Wilhelm Bøchman (ed.) <u>Guds gave vårt kall</u> (Oslo: Norges kristelige studenterbevegelse, 1959), p. 22. See pp. 20–23 for student response to the Group's evangelism in Norway.

[63]Carl Fredrik Engelstad (ed.), <u>Fredrik Ramm</u> (Oslo: Land og kirke, 1946), p. 17.

NOTES

Chapter Three

[1]Hebrews 4:12 (RSV)

[2]"Opgjør med Oxford," VII (June, 1935), 514.

[3]Oslo Arbeiderbladet, June 18, 1935; Janus, op. cit., pp. 524–528.

[4]Meninger (Oslo: Aschehoug, 1947), 144–166.

[5]Oxford Groups: en eiendommelig verdensvekkelse (Oslo: Lutherstiftelsens forlag, 1933), p. 66.

[6]Oxfordbevegelsen i luthersk belysning (Oslo: Norges Lutherlags forlag, 1934), 105.

[7]For fattig og rik, XXVII (July, 1935), 5.

[8]"Gruppebevegelsen som sporsmål til kirken," Norsk Kirkeblad, XVI (August, 1935), 364–371. See also Hans Ording's article, "Oxfordbevegelsen og prestene," ibid., XV (November, 1934), 117–134; letter of Sigmund Mowinckel, Feb. 23, 1961.

[9]Remaking the World, op. cit., pp. 35–37.

[10]R. Selvig in Tidens Tegn, Nov. 27, 1935.

[11]Norsk Kirkeblad, XIV (March, 1935), 123–126.

[12]"Oxfordbevegelsen-mønster eller kraftkilde?" Kirke og Kultur, XLII (June, 1935), 1–24.

[13]Fra Hans Nielsen Hauge til Eivind Berggrav (Oslo: Gyldendal, 1956, p. 113.

[14]Bergen Dagen, June 25, 1935.

[15]Elected in 1928 at the age of thirty-three, he held the position until 1921. See George Brochman, Den norske Forfatterforening gjennom 50 år (Oslo: Den norske forleggerforening, 1952), pp. 266–275, Dagen og veien, op. cit., pp. 143–173, and Tidens Tegn, July 27, 1932, p. 7, for information concerning his activity in the post.

[16]Som det gikk og som det kunde ha gått (Oslo: Gyldendal, 1935), Collected Works, Vol. 9, pp. 182–183; 189–190; 195 and 242.

[17]Dagbladet, Nov. 23, 1935. For other reviews see Nationen and Morgenbladet, Nov. 23 and 28, 1935.

[18]Letter to the investigator dated July 8, 1961. Buchman died the following month on August 7, Time, LXXVIII (August, 1961), 59.

[19]Dated Feb. 16, 1961. In a letter dated March 2, 1961, Helge Krog discloses a similar attitude.

[20]På bar bunn (Oslo: Gyldendal, 1936), Collected Works, vol. 5. I am indebted to Bjarne Berulfsen, professor at the University of Oslo, for the translation (letter dated Nov. 26, 1962).

[21]Dagbladet, Sept. 29, 1936.

[22]Arbeiderbladet, Oct. 2, 1936; Aftenposten, Sept. 26, 1936; Morgenposten, Sept. 30, 1936.

[23]Allerede nu (Oslo: Gyldendal, 1937), Collected Works, vol. 6.

[24]op. cit., p. 156.

[25]Norges litteratur: fra 1914 til 1950 årene, op. cit., pp. 146–147.

[26]Dagbladet, Oct. 29, 1937. See also Kristian Elster's review in Aftenposten, Oct. 29, 1937, and Eugenia Kielland's review in Morgenposten, Oct. 29, 1937.

[27]Borgerfesten (Oslo: Gyldendal, 1939), Collected Works, vol. 7.

[28]Ralph H. Long, et al. (eds.), The Lutheran World Almanac and Encyclopedia 1934–1937 (New York: The National Lutheran Council, 1937), VIII, 22.

[29]Karen Larsen, A History of Norway (Princeton: Princeton University Press, 1950), p. 102.

[30]Ibid., p. 526; Bjarne O. Welder (ed.), Årbok for den norsk kirke (Oslo: Land og Kirke, 1957).

[31]Acts, chapter 9; Paulus og vår egen tid (Oslo: Gyldendal, 1936), pp. 14, 15, 18/27.

[32]"Opstandelse," Tidens Tegn, April 11, 1936.

[33]"Vår kors og kristi kors," April 4, and "Hvad kreves det av en moderne salmebok?," Aug. l.

[34]Bergen Dagen, May 23, 1946.

[35]Ringsaker Menighetsblad, Jan., 1940, pp. 1–2. While living at Dusgård, he attended worship services at the Ringsaker Church.

[36]Elert, op. cit., pp. 321–324.

[37]Article XXIV, The Book of Concord, op. cit., p. 56.

[38]Ringsaker Menighetsblad, op. cit., p. 2; Bergen Dagen, Nov. 11, 1939, p. 6.

[39]Bergen Dagen, op. cit., p. 6.

[40]Tidens Tegn, Feb. 5, 1937.

[41]Bergen Dagen, June 13, 1936.

[42]Norsk Kirkeblad, Oct. 23, 1936, pp. 513–515, Kristen enhet (Oslo; Gyldendal, 1937). The sub-title is entitled "The Group Movement's Ecumenical Message." In an interview on March 3, 1958 Fjelberg spoke about the power of the personal appeal of his colleagues.

[43]"Kirken-sett innenfra og utenfra," Kirke og kultur, LXV (May, 1938), 257–273.

[44]"Den kristen internasjonale," Tidens Tegn, March 25, 1938.

[45]Tidens Tegn, Feb. 27, 1940.

[46]Kristendommen og vår tid (Oslo: Gyldendal, 1938).

[47]Ibid., pp. 5–8; Carl Fredrik Engelstad (ed.), Fredrik Ramm (Oslo: Land og kirke, 1946), pp. 19–20.

[48]The Book of Concord, op. cit., pp. 558–563.

[49]Ibid., pp. 100–107.

[50]Elert, op, cit., p. 69.

[51]Elseth, op. cit., p. 155.

[52]T.S. Eliot, The Idea of a Christian Society (New York: Harcourt Brace, 1940), p. 86.

[53]Krig og kristen tro (Oslo: Gyldendal, 1940).

[54]Oscar Cullmann, The State in the New Testament (New York: Charles Scribner's Sons, 1958), pp. 4–5, 91.

[55]Engelstad, op. cit., pp. 174–175.

[56] Krig og kristen tro, op. cit., pp. 75–76.

NOTES

Chapter Four

[1]Ronald Fangen (ed.), <u>Christian Witness to Our Time, Scandinavian Sermons</u> (<u>Kristent budskap til vår tid</u>, <u>Nordisk prekener</u> Oslo: Gyldendal, 1939), p. l.

[2]"Vidnesbyrd om aanden," <u>Tidens Tegn</u> May 11, 19 40. In an interview with Solveig Fangen on April 23, 1961, she pointed out that the picture of her husband in Engelstad, <u>op</u>. <u>cit</u>., p. 175, shows him assisting a clandestine radio broadcast originating from Hamar. The date was April 14, 1940, and, with German units already in Elverum, the broadcast attempted to rally Norwegian resistance.

[3]"Verdens dom-og Gudsrikets," <u>Urd</u>, June 29, 1940, pp. 758–761.

[4]Ringsaker <u>Menighetsblad</u>, June 1, 1940, pp. 1–2.

[5]<u>Tidens Tegn</u>, Sept. 21, 1940.

[6]"Om troskap," <u>Kirke og kultur</u>, XLVII (October, 1940), 88–97. The article was widely read, Engelstad, <u>op</u>. <u>cit</u>., p. 178.

[7]Interview with Odd Eidem, Jan. 30, 1958; letter from Eidem dated Feb. 9, 1961.

[8]Interview, April 23, 196l. The date of the arrest is taken from Engelstad, <u>op</u>. <u>cit</u>., p. 180. According to the journalist Halvdan Hydle, who was also imprisoned during the occupation, the Germans took their prisoners first to Møllergaten 19, then to the cellar at the Victoria Terrace police station, and then to the Grini concentration camp located not far from Oslo, or to Germany; interview, Feb. 7, 1958.

[9]Interviews, Eivind Berggrav, Oct. 4, 1957; Øivind Berggrav, Feb. 18, 1958; May 2, 1961; Sverre Riisøen, June 29, 1961. See also <u>Kirke og kultur</u>, LI (October, 1946), 440. He was also suspected of having received illegal news bulletins, Oslo <u>Our Land</u> (<u>Vårt Land</u>), March 9, 1946, p. l.

[10]Letter to Solveig Fangen, Nov. 8, 1940; Engelstad, <u>op</u>. <u>cit</u>., p. 179.

[11]Letter to Solveig Fangen from Cell 478, Nov. 19, 1940.

[12]Letter from Solveig Fangen April, 1958. She included a letter from a German official, Herr Grossmann, dated Nov. 23, 1940, in which Fangen was refused permission to attend the funeral. <u>Kirke og kultur</u>, LI (October, 1946), 480.

[13]Letter to Solveig Fangen, Dec. 12, 1940.

[14]Letter to Solveig Fangen, Dec. 15, 1940. Fangen had not anticipated the reaction which followed "Om troskap," as Vagn Riisager maintained in Copenhagen <u>Christian Daily News</u> (<u>Kristelige Dagbladet</u>), Sept. 29, 1946. Contrary to

rumors, Fangen had not been denied a Bible, Oslo Morgenbladet, Feb. 12, 1941. Letter to Solveig Fangen, Dec. 20, 1940.

[15]Solveig Fangen.

[16]Letter to Solveig Fangen, Dec. 28, 1940.

[17]Interview with Eivind Berggrav, Oct. 4, 1957; Kirke og kultur, LI (October, 1946), 481; XLIX (March, 1942), 129–130.

[18]Carl Fredrik Engelstad (ed.), Fredrik Ramm (Oslo: Land og Kirke, 1946), p. 23.

[19]Interview, Jan. 20, 1961. Lundby said he saw the poem "Pasjon" in Ullevål. Rumors in Sweden were that Fangen suffered from a mental collapse. See Sven Stolpe, Fem norrmän, op. cit., p. 176. Other rumors in Norway held that the Gestapo had mistreated him, Oslo Morgenbladet, Feb. 12, 1941.

[20]Letter in possession of Solveig Fangen.

[21]Letter to Solveig Fangen, Feb. 25, 1941.

[22]Dated June 13 and 14, 1941.

[23]Engelstad, op. cit., p. 180; interview with Øivind Berggrav, Feb. 18, 1958.

[24]Interview with Solveig Fangen on a visit to Dusgård, April 24, 1961.

[25]Letter to Harald Hille, June 13, 1942. For an indication of the condition of Fangen's health upon his release from prison, see the photographs in Engelstad op. cit., pp. 177, 179.

[26]Letter to Harald Hille, Sept. 24, 1942; Letter to Stephan Tschudi, July 12, 1942. The novel was presumably The Pastor (Presten) (Oslo: Gyldendal, 1946), Part II of Kvernen som maler langsomt, op. cit., Collected Works, vol. 7.

[27]July 12, 1942.

[28]Ibid., Article XIII, "Apology of the Augsburg Confession," The Book of Concord, op. cit., pp. 211–214; Letter to Stephan Tschudi, July 12, 1942.

[29]Interview with Solveig Fangen, April 23, 1961.

[30]Interviews with Alex Johnson, Jan. 18, 1958; Odd Eidem, Jan. 30, 1958; Carl Fredrik Engelstad, Feb. 20, 1958; Johan Hygen, Nov. 16, 1957, and Einar Lundby, Jan. 20, 1961.

[31]Carl Fredrik Engelstad (ed.) Fredrik Ramm, op. cit., p. 17.

[32]Letter to Harald Hille, April 11, 1942.

[33]Letter from Odd Eidem, Feb. 9, 1961; interview, Jan. 30, 1958.

[34]Oslo Our Land (Vårt Land), Nov. 29, 1945; interview with Sten Bugge, Sept. 25, 1957.

[35]Interview with Alex Johnson, Jan. 18, 1958.

[36]Letter to Lyder Brun, Nov. 18, 1942, Handskriftssal, University of Oslo Library; interview with Harald Hille, March 13, 1961.

[37]To Stephan Tschudi, March 3, 1943.

[38]Ibid. Under the leadership of Manfred Bjorkquist, the Sigtuna Foundation seeks to interpret the Gospel to new conditions of cultural and social life. See Erwin L. L Lueker (ed.), Lutheran Cyclopedia (St. Louis: Concordia Publishing House, 1954), p. 1022.

[39]From an undated mimeographed sheet, in possession of Stephan Tschudi, which Fangen wrote for distribution during the occupation. Interview with Tschudi, June 22, 1961.

[40]Dated April 12, 1944.

[41]Letter dated Sept. 10, 1944. Werner Elert writes, "Luther himself never gave up the idea of the universality of the church." The Structure of Lutheranism, op. cit., p. 275.

[42]Letters dated Oct. 13, 1943, and Sept. 10, 1944. For information about the China Mission Group see Einar Molland, Fra Hans Nielsen Hauge til Eivind Berggrav, op. cit., pp. 89–94.

[43]Letters dated Jan. 31, 1944 and Sept. 10, 1944.

[44]Letters to Bjarne Hareide, July 4, 16, and August 17, 1943; April 19, 1944.

[45]Elert, op. cit., pp. 339–345.

[46]Letter to a "friend in Asker" (who wishes to remain anonymous) dated July 11, 1944; interview with this friend, March 24, 1961. Fangen wrote an eloquent Christian letter of condolence dated May 11, 1942.

[47]Letter to a "friend in Asker," July 20, 1944. One of the cousins, Carsten, was modeled after Conrad. The other cousin, Harald, was perhaps modeled after his youthful friend Harald Hille; interview with Hille, March 13, 1961.

[48]Letters dated Jan. 19, March 28, and July 8, 1944. He was very grateful for the precious tobacco Hille had secured for him.

[49]Letter to Stephan Tschudi, July 7, 1942.

[50]Letter, April 3, 1945. Interview with Bjarne Høye, editor of Our Land, July 19, 1961.

[51]En lysets engel (Oslo: Gyldendal, 1945, Collected Works, vol. 8). The translation by Dermot McKay, Both Are My Cousins (London: Blandford Press, n.d.), uses the opening words of the novel's first sentence as its title. McKay avoids the biblical superscription, II Corinthians 11:14, and omits two sections, pp. 322–29, and 373–78. An announcement concerning a Norwegian youth who died on the Eastern Front is found in the Oslo Aftenposten, Nov. 15, 1941, p. 2. The issues of Dec. 6 and 8, 1941 describe the "Norse Legion" of volunteers.

[52]Oslo Morgenbladet, Sept. 5, 1945. Philip Houm likens En lysets engel to Arthur Koestler's Darkness at Noon, Oslo Dagbladet, Sept. 1, 1945.

[53]Cyril Eastwood, The Priesthood of All Believers (Minneapolis: Augsburg Publishing House, 1962), pp. 12–13. See Elert, op. cit., pp. 340–351.

[54]Presten (Oslo: Gyldendal, 1946, Collected Works, vol. 7). See Engelstad's postscript to the novel, pp. 475–478.

[55]Kirke og kultur, LI (October, 1946), pp. 483–501.

[56]H. Richard Niebuhr, Christ and Culture (New York: Harper and Brothers Publishers, 1951), pp. 45–83.

[57]Kirke og kultur, op. cit., p. 497.

[58]Ibid., p. 496.

[59]Ibid., pp. 498, 501. See also the essay, "Kristendom og moralisme," Tidens Tegn, August 19, 1936.

NOTES

CHAPTER FIVE

[1]Ronald Fangen, Nåderiket, Carl Fredrik Engelstad, editor (Oslo: Gyldendal, 1947), p. 5.

[2]John Bright, The Kingdom of God (New York: Abingdon Press, 1953), p. 7.

[3]I Corinthians 1:21; C.H. Dodd, The Apostolic Preaching and its Development (new edition; London: Hodder and Stoughton, Ltd., 1960), p. 7–8.

[4]Ronald Fangen., Om frihet, Carl Fredrik Engelstad, editor (Oslo: Gyldendal, 1947).

[5]Letter to Stephan Tschudi, October 16, 1943.

[6]Oslo Vårt Land, Dec. 29, 1945. "Tro", an unpublished manuscript in possession of Engelstad, discusses faith in terms of Christian hope.

[7]Letters to Stephan Tschudi, June 30, 1945 and May 7, 1946; interview with Arne Fjelberg, March 3, 1958.

[8]"Referat fra representantmøte" ("Minutes from the Board of Directors"), twenty mimeographed sheets from Vårt Land files provided by Bjarne Høye, dated Jan. 9, 1946.

[9]"Situasjon og oppgave," Vårt Land, No. 1, Aug. 31, 1945, pp. 3–4. In an interview on July 19, 1961, Bjarne Høye stated that Fangen had supported the establishment of Vårt Land. See Fangen's endorsement in a pamphlet from Vårt Land files, "Uttalelser av kjente menn og kvinner om det kristelige dagblad i Oslo og dets oppgaver" ("Statements of Well-Known Men and Women Concerning the Christian newspaper in Oslo and its Tasks"), 14 pp. n. d.

[10]"Referat fra representantsmøte," op. cit., It was decided that the dispute should be resolved at the forthcoming meeting of the newspaper's "Generalforsamling" ("General Assembly") on May 21, 1946.

[11]Vårt Land, Sept. 24, 1945. In an interview on Nov. 14, 1957, a leader of the Kristelig folkeparti, Erling Wikborg, stated that Fangen had urged him to enter politics for the sake of Christian conviction.

[12]"Lyset", an unpublished manuscript in possession of Engelstad; "Kristendom og politikk", Folkets fremtid, I (March, 1945), p. 7; and an essay manuscript (untitled) in possession of Engelstad.

[13]Letter dated October 16, 1943.

[14]Letter to Harald Hille, May 9, 1946.

[15]Interview, September 25, 1957. In interviews with Bjarne Høye on July 19 and 24, 1961, he explained that Fangen's view concerning the propriety of Vårt

<u>Land</u> carrying movie and theatre advertisements was partially adopted: the newspaper would review selected movies and dramas, but it would not accept paid advertisements.

[16]Interview, March 3, 1958.

[17]Interview, January 30, 1958; letter dated February 9, 1961.

[18]R. Biong, <u>et al</u>., "The D.N.L. Ju-52 Crash May 22, 1946," mimeographed report in possession of Hans Kiaer; interview with Kiaer, February 24, 1961. For a complete list of the passengers see Oslo newspapers of May 23, 1946.

[19]Interview, February 24, 1961.

[20]Oslo newspapers, May 23, 1946. The conclusion reached by the Commission was that water in the gas tank caused the sudden loss of power in the left engine and was the probable cause of the crash, Biong,<u>op. cit</u>.

[21]<u>Ibid</u>., May 27 and 28, 1946.

[22]<u>Kirke og kultur</u>, (LXVI, 1939), p. 177.

[23]See the special issue of <u>Kirke og kultur</u>, (LXX, April, 1965). Johan B. Hygen writes, "In the years since his all too early death on many occasions Christians in Norway have thought: At this point we miss Ronald Fangen! But the loss will not becloud the gratitude," p. 226.

[24]<u>Ibid</u>.

[25]T. S. Eliot, <u>The Complete Poems and Plays</u> (Harcourt, Brace and Company, Inc., 1952), p. 56.

[26]<u>Luther's Correspondence</u>, trans. and ed. Preserved Smith and Charles M. Jacobs, Volume II,pp. 176–77.

[27]<u>Perspective on Man</u> (Philadelphia: The Westminster Press, 1961), p. 15.

SELECTED BIBLIOGRAPHY

✦

(The writings of Ronald Fangen)

Allerede nu. Oslo: Gyldendal Norsk Forlag, 1937.

Borgerfesten. Oslo: Gyldendal Norsk Forlag, 1939.

Both Are My Cousins. Trans. Dermot McKay. London: Blandford Press, Ltd., n.d.

Dagen og veien. Oslo: Gyldendal Norsk Forlag, 1934.

De svake. Kristiania: Helge Ericksen, 1915.

Den forjættede dag. Oslo: Gyldendal Norsk Forlag, 1926.

Det nye liv. Oslo: Gyldendal Norsk Forlag, 1935.

Duell. Oslo: Gyldendal Norsk Forlag, 1932.

Duel. Trans. Paula Wiking. New York: The Viking Press, 1934.

En kristen verdensrevolusjon. Oslo: Gyldendal Norsk Forlag, 1935.

En kvinnes vei. Oslo: Gyldendal Norsk Forlag, 1933.

En lysets engel. Oslo: Gyldendal Norsk Forlag, 1945.

En roman. Kristiania: Helge Ericksen, 1918.

Fienden. Oslo: Gyldendal Norsk Forlag, 1922.

Krig og kristen tro. Oslo: Gyldendal Norsk Forlag, 1940.

Krise. Kristiania: Helge Ericksen, 1919.

Kristen budskap til vår tid. Oslo: Gyldendal Norsk Forlag, 1939.

Kristen enhet. Oslo: Gyldendal Norsk Forlag, 1937.

Kristendom og vår tid. Oslo: Gyldendal Norsk Forlag, 1938.

Mannen som elsket rettferdigheten. Oslo: Gyldendal Norsk Forlag, 1934

Nåderiket. Oslo: Gyldendal Norsk Forlag, 1947.

Nogen unge mennesker. Oslo: Gyldendal Norsk Forlag, 1929.

Om frihet. Oslo: Gyldendal Norsk Forlag, 1947.

På bar bunn. Oslo: Gyldendal Norsk Forlag, 1936.

Slægt and slægt. Kristiania: Helge Ericksen, 1916.

Som det gikk og som det kunde ha gått. Oslo: Gyldendal Norsk Forlag, 1935.

Streiftog i digtning og taenkning. Kristiania: Helge Ericksen, 1919.

Syndefald. Oslo: Gyldendal Norsk Forlag, 1920.

Tegn og gjærninger. Oslo: Gyldendal Norsk Forlag, 1927.

Vor Verden. (ed). 8 vols. Oslo, 1923–1930.

English Translations

Both Are My Cousins. (En lysets engel) Trans. Dermot McKay. London: Blandford Press, Ltd., n.d.

Duel (Duell). Trans. Paula Wiking. New York: The Viking Press, 1934.

Stewart D. Govig (1927–2005) was an ordained Lutheran pastor, a Fulbright scholar and a Professor of Religion at Pacific Lutheran University in Tacoma, Washington for 45 years. He was the author of three previously published non-fiction books.

978-0-595-35441-2
0-595-35441-6